5,95

I WONDER WHAT
NOAH
DID WITH THE
WOODPECKERS

I WONDER WHAT

NOAH

DID WITH THE

WOODPECKERS

PROMISE
PRESS
An Imprint of Barbour Publishing

Published by Promise Press, an imprint of Barbour Publishing, Inc., P.O. Box 719, Uhrichsville, Ohio 44683, http://www.barbourbooks.com

Member of the
Evangelical Christian
Publishers Association

Printed in the United States of America.

ACKNOWLEDGMENTS

First things first. Some handshakes and hugs are in order to some fine people—great Americans all—who helped me with this, my first book.

One very special person is my wife Alison. Thanks, sweetheart, for helping me find time to write and for your love and devotion to our family.

I would like to thank my three children, Wriley Hope, Wesley Hardin, and Walker Houston, for providing me with plenty of material and lots of love and laughter.

Thanks to fellow authors Becky Freeman, Chip MacGregor, and Phil Callaway for being such an encouragement.

My friend Randall Murphree deserves a big thank you for being the first to read and edit this material. I never will forget your words, Randall. I believe you said: "And you call this a book?! Unbelievable what passes for literature these days," or something to that effect. Anyway, it meant a lot to me.

Thanks also to my mom and dad for loving and caring for me despite the fact that I was born naked. I love you both dearly.

Finally, I would like to thank Jesus Christ for

saving me from my sins and giving me a new life of hope and peace. If you would like to read what Jesus can and will do for you, please read the Gospel of John.

INTRODUCTION

A merry heart makes a cheerful countenance.

Proverbs 15:13(NKJV)

I'm writing to you from the state that has had more tornadoes in the last two years than any other state in the country—Mississippi. We Mississippians are proud of this statistic, though, since we are constantly listed "last" in just about everything else. I hope to blow you away with this incredible book, but—just as a way of warning—if I should suddenly stop writing this introduction, you will understand what happened.

Hello, I'm Tim Wildmon and thanks for dropping by. I wrote the book you are about to read. Well, at least you are a potential reader at this point. Where did I come up with such a title, you ask? Well, *I Wonder What Noah Did With the Woodpeckers* seemed somehow representative of the humor we can derive from the Bible. Yeah, you read that right, the Bible. Romance, drama, action, passion, thrills, and humor, you can find it all in the best-seller of all time. Me, I like to laugh and have fun with just about everything, including my Christian faith, which—by the way—I do take seriously.

Please, pause with me for a moment of silence so that I can prove to you I can be serious.

Moment of silence.

Thank you.

(Next time, please close your eyes. I always close mine.)

Now I grew up in a Christian home, a preacher's kid in fact, and personally invited Jesus Christ into my life at summer camp in 1976. In these twenty-two years, I've strayed from the Lord a few times, but He's never once left me. The Good Shepherd loves His sheep and I'm glad to be under His watchful eye. There is nothing more joyful, nothing that gives more peace of mind and spirit, nothing that gives more perspective on life, than following Jesus Christ. He is my Rock.

But when I turned over my life to God, I didn't give up my sense of humor. After all, God created humor. So that's why I've included inside these covers a collection of short stories that will—hopefully— make you both laugh and think. I will not ask you to chew gum at the same time as I don't want you to feel any pressure or stress.

I have a question for you: Which one is more important, laughing at life or pondering its meaning? I don't know. I have no doubt, however, that laughter was given to us by God. In fact, laughter has great physiological benefits to the body and mind. I found this recently in my relentless pursuit of truth (it just happened to be on the front page of the newspaper).

Did you know, for instance—

• Children, on average, laugh about 400 times a day, adults only about 15 times. Scientists who study humor want to know why 385 laughs disappear.

• Laughing is aerobic, providing a workout for the diaphragm and increasing the body's ability to utilize oxygen.

• Laughing increases immunity to infections by instantly increasing a flood of disease-fighting cells and proteins into the blood.

• Brain wave activity changes when we catch the punch line of a joke.

• Frequent laughter helps control pain, lower blood pressure, and relieve stress.

Sounds to me like watching *I Love Lucy* or *Andy Griffith* will do you a lot more good than any Jane Fonda exercise video. And you don't even have to do all that stretching and sweating stuff that causes you to grunt and moan due to much pain and unnatural positioning.

Now, keeping things in perspective, there are inappropriate times for laughter. Take ol' Sarah over there in Genesis 18 for instance. The Lord told an aging

Abraham that his not-so-young-and-spry wife Sarah would give birth to a child. Sarah overheard this and laughed. When the Lord confronted her about it, she basically said, "Who, me? It wasn't me who laughed."

And the Lord basically said, "Yes, you did. You laughed at My promise to give you a son. Remember who you're talking to here, Sarah. Think." The point Sarah would make here if she could speak to us today would be: it's okay to laugh with God, just don't laugh at Him.

Now if I were you—and I'm not, so let's get that out of the way during this introduction—I would want to know when the author—which is me—is going to answer the most intriguing question: the reason for the title of this most fascinating and fun-filled book. What *did* Noah do with the woodpeckers? Like any good writer worth his salt, I will wait until the end of the book to deal with this question about my man Noah. So hang in there, people, you'll get your answer later. Now you're on your honor here. I can't, like, keep you from turning to the back right now or anything. Obviously, you've already figured out that I'm not there—or here— with you to physically prevent you from cheating and going straight to the end of the book. No. Nor would I want to. All I can do is appeal to the better side of your nature. Simply, I ask you to respect my wishes as a serious literary artist and read the book from front to back just like I wrote it, savoring the richness of the wisdom contained here in a line by line by line fashion. It's like connecting dots really. Soak it in. Eat it up. Let it clog your main, descending funny-bone artery.

I will tell you one other important note about this book. If you read it backward, you will find hidden messages in code. I'm not sure exactly where yet, because I've outsmarted myself on this one and hidden the secret messages from myself which—I suppose— makes me a genius. Anyway, if you can figure it out, the code will tell you what team will win the World Series in the year 2002. This, of course, will be pointless if there is no world around in which to have a World Series in, as some of my colleagues have predicted (you know, the ones who make millions writing about such end-of-time matters).

Well, I hope you enjoy *I Wonder What Noah Do Did With the Woodpeckers*. I certainly enjoyed writing it. Go on and turn the page and I'll introduce you to some people and also some crazy experiences God has used to teach me some very valuable lessons about life.

In the meantime, I'll keep an eye out for any tornadoes.

Off the Record

"Oh, thanks, mister,
let me handle it!
Blame it all on me!"

–Eve to Adam

Love Must Be
Show-and-Tell

I once heard a speaker on relationships say what men mean by good communication are the headlines and what women look for in quality communication is the fine print.

What is it about the male sex that makes us have a difficult time expressing—or at least verbalizing—ourselves? Generally, we have trouble with everything from the small things, like what happened at work, to larger matters such as love and affection toward other people. Often, we even have trouble expressing ourselves to God.

One night my then five-year-old son Wesley and I were lying in bed as the family was winding down—ever so slowly—for bedtime. I don't want to mislead you into thinking our family is superreligious—because we're not—but one thing we do try to do each evening is pray with the children. We don't always make it there, but when we do I normally ask Wriley, our daughter, to go first, then Wesley, then Mom, and then me. Well, Wesley's usual response to my request for him to pray is a low, barely audible, "I don't want to." (And you thought I was going to quote him as saying something sweet and profound.) No real reason, just, "I don't want to."

One night I told him his Pa Pa Wildmon was an ordained minister of the gospel and that he—Wesley—had no choice but to pray at least seven minutes in King James English. To which Wesley responded, "I'm onlyth fiveth and my vocabulary is not that goodeth." I letteth him slideth that night. (By the way, this King James guy. Did he die of cotton mouth or did he choke to death on his own swollen tongue? Nobody can talk like that without carrying around bottled water.)

Now Wesley doesn't mind holding hands and he doesn't mind closing his eyes but he, unlike Wriley who can pray for everybody and everything, amen, doesn't like verbalizing a prayer. But then, when I call home he doesn't like talking on the phone either, unlike Wriley who will talk about everybody and everything, amen. I've found, with rare exception, males are like this.

Do you remember calling home from college?

Who was the one that wanted to talk most and ask lots of questions? It was Mom, right? Dads generally just want to know if the oil has been changed in the car and if you are studying. One is a yes/no question and the other is relative. Until the grades arrive home anyway.

I am this way with my wife Alison on the phone. She wants to ask me about this, that, and the other, and she wants some detailed information. She wants to know what I think, what's best, my reaction, and my feelings. To which I usually respond, "I don't know, babe, do what you want."

Often when she knows I'm not half paying attention, she'll put me on the spot. "What did I just say to you?" she'll ask.

Usually I try to piece together something which comes out as convoluted nonsense. It could go something like this:

"You said go pick up Wesley at church Thursday night at eleven o'clock after gymnastics and bring home seventy dollars worth of pizzas from Taco Bell."

To which she responds, "I knew you weren't listening to me. You need help. Now, Tim, I can't run this family all by myself, so you better listen to me or it's going to be unpleasant for all of us, especially you. Do you hear me?"

To which I reply, "I don't know, babe, do what you want." (Ha! Ha! This is a joke, ladies. Please, lighten up.)

But on this particular night Wesley and I were alone for a couple of minutes and I asked him if we could pray. When I asked him if he would pray, he said yes. *We're making progress here,* I thought. So we both closed our eyes and I held his hand. Waiting, I said, "You can go first." He squinted and said softly, "Dear God, um (ten seconds of silence here), um, dear God, um. . .I don't really have anything to say." So I gave him a few simple words, which he repeated, we said good night, and off to sleep he went.

For some reason it seems boys and men find it difficult to verbally express affection and love to others. Wesley will one day outgrow his inability to say a prayer, but we all, especially men, need to get past whatever it is that keeps us from telling those around us how we feel about them. Yes, we need to demonstrate love to our wives, our family, and to God—but they also need to hear it from us and hear it often.

The way I see it, if we can slap each other on the rear end after a great play on the football field or baseball diamond, often in front of thousands of people and sometimes on national television without an ounce of shame or embarrassment, we ought to be able to tell those who matter most how we feel, right? In fact, most of these men get paid millions of dollars to—among other things—pat each other on the buttocks. (Not to carry this out too far, but you know you've played a good game if your bottom's sore when the game's over. The better you play, the more slaps on the rear you get from your teammates.) So, what about it, men?

Say it with me, guys, say it out loud, "How 'bout them Cowboys!" Wait a minute, that just came out of nowhere, let me try again. Let's say it together, "I love you." That's it, say it again, only louder and pretend you're looking your wife, child, or your own dad right in the eye. "I love you." You're catching on. Now you can send me the money you were going to send Gary Smalley for those videotapes. (Who needs relationship gurus when you've got the kind of advice you'll find right here in Dr. Tim's first book? Man, I love putting people back together!)

How often do we tell God that we love Him? Do we demonstrate that love with our lives? How often do we tell our wives that we love them, and show that love to be genuine with our actions? The same with our children and others around us.

Jesus set the standard for us. He told His disciples

He loved them and then He proved it. Indeed, words are cheap if they are not backed up with actions. But then again, there are no more powerful words in the world than, "I love you." So let me encourage you to do as Wesley will be doing in school this fall: play a little show-and-tell. In your case, try doing it with those you love and care for.

These Three Things

1. Jesus said, "This is My commandment, that you love one another as I have loved you" (John 15:12 NKJV).

2. The people whom we love with our actions, also need to be told they are cherished and loved.

3. King James should be remembered as a cruel ruler for inflicting such a language on his people. Why couldn't he have had the Bible translated into plain, southern English, y'all?

OFF THE RECORD

"You're kidding me,
right?"

–Goliath to David

Direction Makes
a Difference

Ever since I can remember I have been a sports
fanatic. I've loved playing and watching football, basketball, and baseball since I was a kid. The older I get
the more I enjoy watching and the less I enjoy playing,
or so says my body.

When I was eight years old I used to carry around
a transistor radio and listen to the St. Louis Cardinals
all summer. WELO in Tupelo—580 on the AM dial
—carried all the games. When the Cardinals played
on the West Coast the radio went to bed with me for
those midnight finishes against the Dodgers, Padres,
or Giants. I loved everything about the broadcast with
the legendary Jack Buck and sidekick Mike Shannon.
From "The Dugout Show" to the "Star of the Game,"
I didn't miss a play or an interview. I knew everything
about the Cardinals. Batting averages, ERAs, Lou

Brock's number of stolen bases, you name it. Baseball, bike riding, swimming, and the Cardinals on radio—that was my life in the summer of 1971. Richard Nixon was president and summer lasted forever. Life was simple. Life was sweet. I miss those days.

It was about that time my dad began taking me to Mississippi State football games. I became a loyal fan of the Bulldogs, learning a lesson in humility (and humiliation) every time MSU played the legendary Alabama teams of Coach Bear Bryant. The Lord gave Moses eleven commandants, you know. The lost one read: "And thou, University of Alabama, shalt never lose to Mississippi State in football." Actually, Moses took it upon himself to scratch #11, as he did not think the Israelites would understand the religious experience that is college football in the South.

My affection for sports has remained a big part of my life. In fact, to this day, the first part of the newspaper I read each morning is the sports section. If some third-world dictator nukes us, it will have to wait until I'm finished reading how Troy Aikman did against the Redskins. It's pitiful, I know.

I'll be the first to admit that from time to time this love for sports gets a little out of hand. For instance, I talked my bride, Alison, into going to St. Louis for our honeymoon. Now hold on there, ladies, it's not what you might think. I mean, sure we took in three Cardinal games, but we also went to the Arch, the world famous zoo, and Six Flags. And what could be more romantic than going down the "Screaming Eagle" hand in hand?

Now my oldest son Wesley, much to his dad's pleasure, is beginning to show an interest in sports. Soccer, however, just wasn't his bag. In fact, he told me that very thing one afternoon after one of those soccer doodads. Matches, I think they call them.

"Dad, soccer just isn't my bag," he said, hoping I wouldn't get upset with him.

"Son, that's all right," I said as I bent down on one knee, placed my hands on Wesley's shoulders, and looked him squarely in the eye. "Listen to me, Wes, and I'll tell you what my dad told me and what his dad told him. We're Americans, Wes. And real, red-blooded, hamburger eatin', stick-your-own-worm-on-the-hook Americans, well, we don't believe in sports where you can't use your hands. If a man can't use his hands, the game ain't worth playin', son. Always remember your daddy told you that."

Little did I know what a stir this would create when Wesley started telling all his friends they were wimps for playing soccer. "My dad said you were against America," Wesley preached to other kids.

And their parents got mad at me! Why? For simply telling my son how to be a good American! Can you believe it? Some people are so touchy when it comes to their kids.

Anyway, I decided to let him try T-ball. Meanwhile, I would take my coaching skills, gleaned from church league softball, onto the T-ball field.

Before I go any further, let me say that, yes, the rumors are true—my church league coaching record is no wins in three years. We were 0 for 1992, '93, and '94. For the record, I really never had any material to work with. My guys—the laughingstock of the league—were the Bad News Bears twenty years later. On a "good" day, our team was very, very bad. On other days we ranged anywhere from absolutely pitiful to completely inept to embarrassingly pathetic. My pastor once told me, "Tim, I'm sorry to bring this up, but word is getting around town how bad your softball team is and quite frankly—you're killing church visitations."

To which I responded, "I spend two months getting this team together, risk life and limb playing catcher for these bozos, even bring the Gatorade, and keep that depressing score book and this—this is the thanks I get? Thanks a lot, Brother Tender Heart."

He said he didn't care about all that, asked that I disband the team, and said the church would even pick up the cost of our jerseys so that they could be burned. I took this hard and pleaded with him to let me finish the season with what little dignity I had left, which is what I did.

From the day I told Wesley I was going to coach his T-ball, he kept asking me about every other day when we were going to start. "Soon, son," I would tell him.

"Does that mean tomorrow, the day after tomorrow, or the day after that?" he would ask. (This was several weeks before our first practice.) Finally, our first practice arrived one Saturday morning in late April.

Now, keep in mind here, these twelve kids (five- and six-year-olds) were rookies of the first order. None of them had a shred of experience in organized baseball. I only knew three or four of them, they didn't know me, and most of them didn't know each other. I sat down on third base and motioned for them to gather around. I gave everyone a piece of gum to calm their little nerves, we had a short prayer, and we started talking baseball. We talked and then we practiced—if you can call it that—for about an hour.

One field over was another team coached by Henry Littlehaus, a friend of mine. Or so I thought. It was probably their third or fourth practice and they were already a well-oiled machine. They were color-coordinated, well-equipped, and seemed unusually disciplined for their age. In other words, if this were a scene in a movie, my friend would be Arnold Schwarzenegger and I would be Woody Allen.

On our water break Henry challenged me—in front of my players, no less—to a short game. "Yeah, coach, let's play them!" a few of my players said to me. I eyed my "friend" with a, "You are a lowlife" look. He didn't care. He was out to embarrass me.

What was I supposed to say? "No, kids, we're going to work on the fundamentals," would make it seem like I was ducking from a challenge. It also sounded boring. I remember when I was a kid I wanted to play, not practice. So I decided to take a step on the wild side and let my team play after a full one hour of practice. We took our gear next door and I explained to my team what "on deck" meant and told them to listen to their base coach. *Oh well, you learn by doing,* I thought to myself.

My first two batters did okay, hitting the ball and running to first base. *This is going pretty well,* I thought with a grin. Then my third batter, Robert, came to the plate. The little guy took a good whack, hit the ball, and began to run his heart out. He was fast, too, he was really "diggin' it," as we say in baseball circles. Yes sir, my little man was runnin' hard. There was only one problem. The lil' fellow was running to third base, not first, a fundamental violation of baseball law.

As you can imagine, the adults—including the little fellow's dad—were bending over in laughter. I couldn't help myself either. I yelled over at Littlehaus, "Hey, Henry, my little man meant to do that just to throw your team off. It worked too, look at your team. They're all just standing around laughing."

"You've got a little work to do there, Wildmon!" he yelled back. "You need to study the rule book more before you ruin these kids for life."

The other team—little "better-than-thou" snobs — got a big kick out of this. However, I really knew I had a long way to go when I looked over at my dugout and saw my little girls and boys yelling for their teammate to keep running to the next base—wherever it was!

Robert's dad went over, bent down, and put his arm around his son, told him what he did wrong and what to do next time, all the while trying to hold back his own laughter.

The basics. The fundamentals. The rules of the game. In the Christian life we often spend a lot of energy blowin' and goin' in the wrong direction, don't we? Many times we do this with the best of intentions, just like children on the T-ball field. But what we really need to do is stop and listen to the Master Teacher through the reading of His word and through prayer. I've been really convicted recently of the importance of these two things. I have asked the Lord for a new hunger for prayer and daily devotional time so that I may know His direction for my life, both generally and day to day. The Lord says if we will seek Him, we will find Him. But how much time do we spend seeking? More time than we spend reading the sports page, I hope. (Ouch!)

Well, needless to say, it was an interesting and entertaining two months of T-ball. I had a blast and so did the kids. My little "wrong way" buddy Robert went the right way the rest of the season and turned out to be one of my best players. Wesley's already asking me about next season.

And, oh yes, the name I chose for our team—the Cardinals, of course, what else? Now let's review that '71 season, shall we?

THESE THREE THINGS

1. God desires that we—like young Robert on the base path—go all out for Him. He want us to listen to His guidance, though, rather than running off in the wrong directions.

2. Followers of Christ need a teachable spirit (Psalm 143:10).

3. For some unknown reason, my church league team did begin to win a few games after I resigned as their coach and moved on to T-ball.

"Yeah,
and I'm Howdy Doody!"

–One Christian to another when told
Saul of Tarsus had been converted

Exact Change Only

In our church we sing a song that goes like this: I owed a debt I could not pay, He paid a debt He did not owe, I needed someone to wash my sins away. And now I sing a brand new song, Amazing grace the whole day long, Christ Jesus paid a debt that I could never pay.

A few years back I was in Philadelphia, Pennsylvania, not to be confused with Philadelphia, Mississippi—I've spoken in both—and trust me, there are very few similarities. They both use asphalt on their roads and that's about it. I was on my way to a speaking engagement about fifty miles north of the city. As I left my hotel in the middle of the afternoon en route to where I would be speaking, I got on a major expressway that wove through the City of Brotherly Love. Now I consider myself above average when it comes to a sense of direction and finding my way, but this time I got off to a bad start. Well, here I go being modest again and we're just in the third chapter. (You'll have to pardon me, I struggle with this.) Actually, I consider myself well above average when it comes to sniffing out the right direction. Map or no map, I'll find my way, thank you, thank you very much.

As I got on the expressway I soon learned that it was the right road, but I was driving in the wrong direction, heading toward New Jersey instead of north. I began to look for an exit, but, before I reached one, I noticed cars were stopped ahead. The reason: a toll bridge. Now tollbooths—invented by mean and evil legislators who probably fly private planes every- where they go—while very common in many parts of the country, are very rare below the Mason-Dixon line. We southerners would rather pay taxes than stop every ten miles for this annoyance. Although Yankees won't admit it, this was one of the conditions the South insisted on to end the Civil War. Standing on the Appomattox, Virginia, courthouse steps that fate- ful day, April 9, 1865, Gen. Robert E. Lee turned to Gen. Ulysses S. Grant, who would later become pres- ident of the United States, and said:

"Ulysses, there's one more thing other than the fact that you should change that crazy first name of yours," said Lee. "When I say it I sound like I've been drinkin'."

"Well, Bob, there's not much I can do about my name," responded Grant. "What else can I help you with?"

"It's the matter of tollbooths. We don't want 'em."

"Well, Bob, you're not in much of a position to negotiate here, but I'll grant the South this one request."

And so—although you won't find this in any historical accounts—the course of American history was changed forever.

As I drew closer to the bridge, which, incidentally, had about fifteen lanes of traffic all packed with rush-hour drivers, I noticed a sign above each of the gates demanding: "Exact change only." All of the signs within my range of vision said the same thing: "Exact change only." I later learned that there were two lanes on the far right that had live bodies to make change. I—for once in my life—was on the far left on an issue and, predictably, it got me in trouble.

What's up with this? I thought. I quickly felt my pockets and my fear became reality; I did not have exact change. It is hard to explain the sinking feeling I had. You see, these gates were operated automatically and there were no attendants—that I could see—to help those who were caught without exact change. There I was with hundreds of

Philadelphia rush-hour drivers packed in behind me and absolutely no place for me to go but forward. So forward I went.

I began to think, *This is not fair to out-of-towners. What am I doing in Philadelphia, Pennsylvania, anyway? I'm a friendly little catfish in a shark pond here! Surely I'm not the first person ever to reach this booth and not have the exact change. What have others done? What am I going to do when I get to the gate and I can't go any further?* I felt nauseous. My palms were clammy, my mouth dry. Frantically I looked over the rental car for change between the car seats, in the glove compartment, in the cassette deck (almost losing two fingers), anywhere. No luck.

After about ten minutes of agonizing I reached the gate. No change. No attendant. No hope, as far as I could determine. Now I ask you, what would you have done? Several ideas (not all of them legal or honest) went through my mind as the cars honked behind me. I could:

1. Burst through the gate à la Burt Reynolds, ask forgiveness later, and hope the cops wouldn't catch me. (Not really a viable option for the vice president of a national Christian ministry.)

2. Get out of the car, go hit the gate, throw my hands up in the air, look at the cars behind me and

yell, "Oh, this is great! The stupid gate is broken! Can you believe it!"

3. Get out of the car and start going down the line behind me—a very embarrassing and humiliating experience indeed—searching for someone who could give change for a dollar: three quarters, two dimes and a nickel, you know.

Embarrassment won out over dishonesty. I went with Idea Number Three. Expecting much verbal abuse, I got out of my car and walked, head down, to the first car behind me. Country come to town.

"Afternoon," I said politely with what I thought was a slight southern accent, holding out George Washington to the driver in the first car behind me, a man in his fifties. The fellow didn't answer. He shook his head as if to say, "You redneck idiot!" and pointed toward an attendant—who could have been an angel as far as I was concerned—making his way down to my car from out of nowhere. I thought about waving to the folks behind us, you know, just to break the tension. Maybe yell to them I was an out-of-towner, hopefully incurring a little under-standing so they wouldn't think me a complete idiot—but I wasn't sure they would be receptive to good ol' southern friendliness at that particular point and time.

As I went toward the attendant, I began to apologize and explained that I was not from the area—when he interrupted, "What's the matter? Can't you read?" in reference to the "Exact change" sign.

Somewhat taken aback by Brother Sunshine, I said, "Yes, I can read," enunciating my words. (I was tempted to whip out a book and start reading to him just to prove it—but I didn't have one handy.) "But I'm from Mississippi and this whole thing just caught me by surprise." When he heard my accent he rolled his eyes. I knew I was not enhancing the image of my state. (Come to think of it, his question didn't do much to enhance the image of his area either.) Anyway, he quickly took my dollar, opened the gate, and I was on my way.

What a relief. What a sense of freedom.

The Bible says the "exact change" for crossing the bridge into heaven—the real City of Brotherly Love—is faith in Jesus Christ. Without Him, we have no hope. No chance of life abundant or life eternal. So if you haven't made that decision to trust Jesus, please don't delay. Believe me, it's a terrible feeling to reach the toll booth without "exact change."

Now sing it with me. You know the tune. I owed a debt I could not pay, He paid a debt He did not owe, I needed someone to wash my sins away. And now I sing a brand new song, Amazing grace the whole day long, Christ Jesus paid a debt that I could never pay.

On second thought, why don't you just hum it.

THESE THREE THINGS

1. "For there is one God and one Mediator between God and men, the Man Christ Jesus" (1 Timothy 2:5 NKJV).

2. Jesus Christ paid the price for our redemption. Trust Him today.

3. When traveling in unfamiliar territory—especially the northeastern part of the U.S.—always carry a sack full of change. (I recommend $100 for every fifty miles.)

"Despite what you have been told,
I was not a bullfrog in a previous
life and I am going to slap
the next person who asks me."

–Jeremiah the prophet

Career Decisions

Did you hear about that smart eleven-year-old? He has an unbelievable IQ. In fact, if you suffer from a severe inferiority complex, you might want to skip to the next chapter and come back to this later.

Have you wondered why God made us all different and unique? I know a lot of people we interact with—or even attend church with—we just look at and think, *Thank God, there's only one.* We question why the Lord placed this person in our path in the first place and are constantly tempted to tell this person to, "Get out of my path." But we know (or we guess or suppose) God has a reason and so we endure many brothers and sisters who grate on our Christian nerves. Sometimes, however, the patience runs thin, doesn't it?

"Listen, I know what the Bible says about sharing your faith," I said once to one of these strange brothers. "But really, I think you would be doing us all a favor if you just didn't mention that you're a Christian or a member of this church when you're out in public, all right?"

Brother Strange gave me a bewildered blank stare.

"Really, I checked with the Lord and He said it was okay by Him. He actually prefers it."

We all know these brothers and sisters, don't we? The one who always greets you with a verse from the Book of Revelation or tells you what the Lord revealed to him about you in a dream the other night. After a night of spicy Mexican food, no doubt. I'm often tempted to return the favor with these folks and tell them some off-the-wall, bizarre request the Lord is making of them through me.

"Yes, brother, it's true," I'd love to say. "I was mowing my yard yesterday and I believe I heard the voice of an angel—tenor I think it was—although I'm not good with music and the mower was awful loud. It was singing regardless. But anyway, the Lord told this angel, male or female I do not know, to tell me to tell you the next time I saw you that you are to go down to Kroger, on Saturday afternoon—it has to be Saturday afternoon, I'm certain about that—and do a three-hour handstand on isle seven. Yeah, I know it'll be a real test of your faith, but seven's God's number, you know. I think that's the baby food aisle so you want to be real careful, okay?"

"Really, Brother Tim? Are you sure?"

"Oh, no question about it. In fact, I wasn't really clear on this one, but I think you're supposed to bark like a dog while you handstand. Yeah, it's coming back to me now. You're to bark like a big dog. Woof! Woof! Just like that. Try it out for me right here one time, will ya?"

"Well, okay. If you think the Lord told you this."

"Oh, absolutely."

"Well. How about. . .woof."

"No, no, brother. Louder. I'm talkin' a pronounced woof. Like this. WOOF! WOOF! WOOF! Now you try it."

"I feel kind of weird here in the church foyer."

"Oh, you're not weird, brother. Go ahead, do it."

"Okay, here goes. WOOF! WOOF! WOOF! WOOF! WOOF! WOOF! WO. . ."

"Good, good. That's. . ."

"WOOF! WOOF! WOOF! WOOF!"

"That's enough, brother. You're doin' fine. Great woof, just great. You're all ready for that Saturday afternoon spiritual handstand. Now go get 'em, Tiger!"

"Okay, Brother Tim. I'll pray about it."

"Oh no, brother. You don't have to pray about it. Just like all the times you've given me a word from the

Lord and I've taken your word for it, you need to trust me on this one. Kroger, Saturday, handstand, woof, that's all you need to know."

"Well. . ."

"Now, I don't know what this all means except that it's a test of your faith and I'm convinced you'll understand why Puff the Magic Dragon lived by the sea and how Batman and Robin fit into the Book of Revelation when you're through. And rest assured, my dear brother, although I can't be there, I'll be handstanding with you in prayer."

Oh, how sweet the thought. Save your letters, 'cause I know I'm not being exactly charitable here—but admit it, you've had the same thoughts at least once in your Christian life.

It takes all kinds in the Body of Christ, I suppose.

Ray Stevens used to sing a song that went "Everything is beautiful in its own way." Although not completely theologically correct, there is still an element of truth in the song. God created man in His own image, the Bible tells us in Genesis. He bestows on every person He grants life to certain gifts, talents, and abilities. (Sometimes it's the gift of mercy for Brother Strange.) But it's up to us to use those gifts. Jesus spoke of this when he told the Parable of the Talents in Matthew 25.

Well, let's talk about eleven-year-old Michael Kearney's talent, the kid I mentioned back at the beginning of this chapter. Michael's from Tennessee and his story appeared in newspapers recently:

Why waste time? Now that eleven-year-old Michael Kearney has graduated from college, he's working on a graduate degree.

All in preparation for becoming a game show host.

"He could be Mozart, Einstein. We have no idea," said Kevin Kearney, father of the boy with the 300 IQ. "Right now he wants to be a game show host. That's a passion we have to accept."

Michael was the youngest child on record to enter college—age 6—and the youngest to graduate—age 10—when he got his degree in anthropology last year at the University of South Alabama.

Now Michael could probably, without much help, turn the computer world upside down with new technology and make people forget about Bill Gates. He could quite likely bring the world's leaders together and solve all international disputes in a day or two. Okay, three. And, for you bottom-line folks, Michael could probably have a net worth of $20 billion within five years. All these are potentially within Michael's grasp.

Instead, Mike wants to be the next Bob Barker. Some kids want to be sports heroes. That was me. Others desire to be astronauts or military leaders. And then there are some who want to grow up and be game show hosts. Hey, that's one of the great privileges of being a kid, having your own dreams.

But I have to tell you, if my son Wesley was the smartest kid on the planet, and he told me he wanted to pursue a career as a game show host, I would be very tempted to let him have a small piece of what little mind he inherited from me. But then, I wonder, how does a dad sit down with a son this intelligent and try to talk some sense into the boy? I mean, you're talking to a kid with a 300 IQ. What do you say? "Now son, I'm not sure your head is screwed on straight here."

Me? If I were in Michael's dad's shoes, and Wesley was touting a 300 IQ, I would probably sit down with my son and with all the calmness and reason I could muster, say something encouraging like this.

"Game show host! Game show host! Your mother and I win the brain lottery and you're telling me you want to be a game show host! Let's see here, Wes, maybe it's me, but a quick name association run-through tells me Albert Einstein and Wink Martindale didn't exactly contribute equally to the human race! A game show host! Listen to your daddy, Wesley, look at me in the eye here. Wes, do you know what kind of money you can bring home to your momma and daddy with your brain? Do you know how happy all that money would make me and your momma, Wesley?

"A game show host! Now Wesley, you leave me and your mother no choice, either you take that screwball idea back about being a game show host, or you will be grounded indefinitely. Look at me when I talk to you, son! Do you understand me? Well, obviously you understand me—you've got a 300 IQ, for goodness sakes. But Wes, we're talking no 'Wheel of Fortune,' no 'Price is Right,' no 'Hollywood Squares,' no nothing! Now go to your room and don't come out 'til you can talk some sense!"

In all seriousness, I wish Michael and his family the best. I'm sure we will be reading about Michael Kearney soon enough. But why God decided to put the brain power of my entire family tree in one little boy, I'll never understand. But then, being your average 110 IQ, there are a lot of things I don't understand.

I do know this, however. God gives us all talents, be they physical, mental, and, for the Christian, spiritual. The Body of Christ needs each Christian to use his or her God-given talents—which is why all of us in the Church need each other. (Believe it or not, we even need Brother Strange!)

And as the three servants learned in the parable, the Master does hold us accountable.

THESE THREE THINGS

1. I am responsible to God for how I utilize the talents and gifts He has blessed me with. (Matthew 25)

2. God uses all kinds of people—even some with very, shall we say, unique, personalities—to make up His Church.

3. I am mentally inferior to an eleven-year-old boy from Tennessee who could soon be my boss.

"You are one stubborn hombre,
you know that?"

–Moses to Pharaoh

SOMETHING FISHY

Fish are the only creatures that continue to grow long after they've been in the deep fry. Have you noticed this? What was once a four-pound bass in 1998 will be a legendary ten-pound bass in 1999. I don't know what it is about men and fishing that we can't seem to resist the temptation to stretch the truth. It kind of makes you wonder if ol' Peter and Andrew didn't tell a few fish stories in their day. Before they met Jesus, of course.

Yes, fishing is therapy for many folks, but it's also very competitive among men. Men take fishing personally. And they usually don't like to give away just "how" and "where" they catch the big ones. And, of course, "big" depends on who catches what fish.

Fishing, more than almost any other human endeavor, takes persistence. A good fisherman needs the right bait, the right equipment, and above all, a lot of patience.

Many times when I've been fishing with my father-in-law Jim, we've found a good spot on the water and begun reeling fish in one after another. But then, when another boat comes by and someone yells over, "Having any luck?" I just kind of shrug my shoulders. "You might try the other end of the lake," I say between pointing and reeling in another nice one. "Good luck." For just a brief second I question the honesty of what I've said. Then, I reason, who knows, there might be even more fish biting at the other end of the lake.

Jesus told Peter and Andrew he would make them fishers of men. Now that's an interesting concept. "Fishing" for the hearts of men and women.

I remember the times Jim and my brother-in-law Russ and I would go camping on the Tombigbee River along the Mississippi-Alabama border. Now, my in-laws liked to have a good time, but they were also very serious about fishing. They were firm believers that if you went on a fishing trip you came back with a nice mess of fish. If not, you had failed the family.

As you can already tell, Jim and Russ were avid outdoorsmen. They loved to hunt and fish for hours, days sometimes. Me, I married into the family. Yeah, I liked fishing and an occasional night under the stars, but I'm more of a house guy. You know, clean sheets, air-conditioning, cable television kind of guy. I really enjoy watching the outdoor shows on TNN though.

When I would go on these overnight excursions, one of the first things we would do is motor up the river until we found a good spot—according to Russ and Jim—to set what we call around here a "trotline." I would chime in, "Yeah. Looks like a good place to me, too." I hadn't a clue, but I wanted to be one of the guys. I did this often. One of them would say, "Looks like turtles have been taking our bait," and I would say, "Yeah, looks like turtles to me."

Now a trotline, for you non-outdoor types (you wimps!), is a long stretch of nylon line that has hooks spaced out about three feet apart, and runs usually about fifty to seventy-five yards across a lake or a river. We put minnows or chicken liver on the fifty or so hooks. You've got to put some sort of weights along the way so that the line will sink a few feet where the fish are. Fish, I have learned, typically go after the bait when it is submerged. (Are you paying attention to me? I'm only going to go over this once as I only have so much space for this story. So sit up straight and pay attention. After all, you don't know what tomorrow holds and this survival skill could very well save your life one day.)

After setting the line and baiting the hooks, we would go back to our campsite and cook or fish or rest or talk. Mostly, we would fight off chiggers. One night I slept without my socks on, in the open air. Chiggers ate me alive. You can't feel the devils bite while you're asleep, but I cried when I awoke. My feet looked like strawberries. I thought I was going to have to amputate my puppies. The itching and burning caused by the eighty-three bites was downright brutal.

Every two hours we would get back in the boat, get the spotlight out, and ride back up the Tombigbee River to carefully "run the trotline" as Jim would say. We would check every hook and if it needed to be rebaited, we rebaited it. But the thrill came when one of us would pick up the line out of the water and feel the tug or jerk that told us—without a doubt—we had caught something. The excitement would intensify as we actually got to see what kind of fish it was and what size. We caught a lot of big catfish and even some large turtles on those trotlines.

The point in telling you this is to say chigger bites burn. Wait a minute, that was not my point. Well, it is a point, but not my main one. Let's see, oh yeah, my primary point here—in this particular paragraph, right here, the one you are now reading—is to say we took our fishing seriously. We had the right bait, we carefully set the hooks, and we kept at it. I don't remember a time when we didn't come home with plenty of fish.

Are we—as followers of Christ—sharing our faith with others so that they may be attracted to the Master? The bait—really—should be our lives. As the saying goes, others should want what we Christians have. They should see Jesus Christ in us through our actions as well as our words.

We should demonstrate love for one another. Love is kind of like a big fat juicy worm. I'll bet you never thought of love like that before you read this, had you? (Please, you need not compliment me, I just have a gift for painting meaningful word pictures.)

Are we serious about telling others the old, old story of Jesus and His love?

Today, I challenge you to let Jesus make you a "fisher of men," for His name's sake.

THESE THREE THINGS

1. Even today, Jesus issues the invitation for us to come, and let Him make us fishers of men. Have you introduced anyone to Christ recently?

2. Our lives should be bait for our friends, family, and coworkers who don't know the Lord.

3. Take it from Tombigbee Tim, trotlines need to be checked at least once every two or three hours. (And always sleep with your socks on!)

OFF THE RECORD

"You'll get to eat soon
enough there, big fellow."

–Daniel

BACKWARDS GRACE

"American by birth, Southern by the grace of God," read the T-shirt I saw on a fellow coming out of Wal Mart in my hometown of Tupelo, Mississippi, the other day. I chuckled. I wonder if in Los Angeles they wear T-shirts that say, "American by birth, West Coast dude by the grace of God." What about in Chicago? Do folks have T-shirts that read, "American by birth, Midwestern Cubs fan by the grace of God?" (I doubt it. Being a lifelong Cardinals fan, I've always considered being a Cubs fan a curse rather than a blessing.) And New York City? Do the young boys playing stickball on the streets of Brooklyn wear T-shirts that read, "American by birth, New Yorker by the grace of God." Possibly. Although, my favorite T-shirt of New York has the big red apple on the front of it that reads, "I Love New York."

Go anywhere in this great land of ours—from New

York to L.A.—and people are proud of their communities, towns, cities, and states. That's the way it should be. People in Oregon take pride in their beautiful state and great people. The same is true of Michigan, Arizona, Kansas, and Maine. There are good and bad people everywhere. One of the benefits of my work and travel is meeting so many brothers and sisters in Christ all over America. One such brother is Brandt Gustavson, president of the National Religious Broadcasters. Brandt, a refined Yankee of many years mostly spent in the *Chicargo* area, is always ribbing me about my roots. "Hey, Tim, now just where is Tupelo, anyway?" he likes to say in front of others. I tell him it's right below one below.

You did read that right, many southerners refer to the Windy City where the Cubs play as "Chicargo." I don't know why we do this. To make matters worse we always want to put the "s" on Illinois which—of course—as the rest of America knows, is silent. "I think Bill had a meetin' in Chicago, Illinoise," is what can be heard on any given day down here. A lot of my fellow southerners also call our nation's capital "Warshington, D.C." Again, I don't know who started this—probably folks in east Tennessee, if I had to blame somebody—but it ain't right and I don't do it and I make it a point to correct folks when I hear it.

But there's something different, southerners would argue something special, about how we so-called rednecks see ourselves. Maybe it's because we've been looked down upon by the rest of the country for some of our "backward" ways. "Oh, they still do that in the Bible Belt," I heard a political commentator say in a condescending way the other day on CNN. Yes, there have been some serious problems associated with our region of country over the years, no question about that, but some recent events that have transpired here have made me proud of this "Bible Belt" land of catfish and grits I call home. And when we have opportunity to crow, we backwards folks can crow with the best of them. So allow me to brag on my neighbors to the east for a few moments.

To the direct east of Mississippi is, of course, the great state of Alabama. (We have a lot of learnin' here in the South and that's how I know these things. I could go ahead and tell you the state to the east of Alabama, but my guess is you're impressed enough with what geography I've laid out already.) Recently, Alison and I loaded up our van and crossed the state line on U.S. 78 headed to Birmingham and then I-65 on down to Montgomery, the state capital, to attend a historic rally in support of religious freedom and America's Christian heritage.

We went though towns like Guwin (which is not to be confused with Gu-win which is right next door), Winfield, where the famous Boars Butt restaurant serves up some very tasty barbeque, and Jasper, where you can get a speeding ticket if you don't slow down real fast coming into town. Trust me, I have fifty dollars worth of personal knowledge of this fact. 1992, I think it was.

The people God used in Alabama—among several —to carry the banner for religious freedom, to fight this fight, included Judge Roy Moore and Gov. Fob James. Judge Moore, who I had the great privilege of meeting and shaking hands with, is a municipal judge in Gadsden who was sued by the American Civil Liberties Union for having the Ten Commandments on his courtroom wall and opening his sessions with prayer. Judge Moore was ordered by another federal judge in Alabama to cease the prayers and take down the Ten Commandments. He said no, he wouldn't do it, said he would rather go to jail, citing the many evidences of America's rich Christian heritage, including the fact that these same Ten Commandments are in fact on both the doors and the wall of the Supreme Court of the United States of America. When and if this case ever makes its way up to this august group of nine justices, I wonder if five of them will decide it's time to take the doors off their hinges and sandblast the wall above their heads?

Several outstanding Americans (including my dad) spoke at the rally my family and I attended on the capital steps. We were joined by 25,000 other God-fearing Americans, some of whom traveled from as far away as Minnesota and California to show their support of these gentlemen and, more importantly, the Constitution of the United States of America. I met "backwards" folks from all over America—not just the South—that afternoon.

It was a great and glorious day. I took the opportunity to share with my three young children why we were there and, as best I could, what it was all about. There is much I could say. The rains that had poured down for the previous twenty-four hours halted and the skies began to clear off just an hour or so before the rally. Perhaps it was God telling us that although the headlines don't look good for our blessed republic these days, maybe with people like Governor James and Judge Moore there is hope after all. I like to think so anyway.

As I got in the driver's seat late that afternoon, the van unusually quiet as Alison and the kids drifted off to sleep, and started back to my beloved Magnolia State, I thought to myself, *You know what, Tim, there's a lot to be said about this Bible Belt region of the country where God and country still mean something.* Yes, we have our problems like anywhere else, but it's nice to know there are still places in America where officials at the highest level of government are willing to stand up to the ACLU and others who would erase our godly heritage. Maybe I'll have a new T-shirt made. Yeah, that's what I need to do. It'll read: American by birth, backwards by the grace of God.

THESE THREE THINGS

1. The Ten Commandments are as relevant today as they were when God gave them to Moses.

2. America needs more men and women of conviction like Judge Roy Moore and Gov. Fob James.

3. The Boars Butt restaurant is a real place in Winfield, Alabama. If you're in the area, stop by and try some of their barbeque.

"I'm warning you, Abel,
stick your straw in my drink
one more time and
you're history."

–Cain

PACHYDERMS AND PRINCIPLES

Did you see recent news accounts about the herd of wild elephants running free in India? It sounds crazy, but it's true. The fifty-member herd of pachyderms trampled people and property for 180 miles. Just one more reason why it's great to be an American. We have our drive-by shootings, yes, but at least we don't have to mess with wild elephants roaming our highways and neighborhoods.

Let's think about this for a moment. If we did have wild elephants roaming our streets, how would the Channel 6 Skycam report this news? It might go something like this:

"Thank you, John. It's busy on roads leading into the city this morning. There's a two-car accident on Lamar Avenue where police are already on the scene. There is also some construction on Union Avenue causing some delays and looking down Winchester it appears the elephants are back, John. Let's see, one, two, three, four, five. . .five, I think we're looking at five wild elephants roaming around just smashing cars and trucks to little pieces. Oooh, that's ugly! Anyway, expect some delays on the east part of town until these big guys move on out. Other than the wild elephants causing much fear and hysteria on Winchester, everything else looks fairly normal in the city. That's your morning report from Channel 6 Skycam. Now back to you, John."

"Alrighty, Bill, thanks for that report. Makes you kind of glad you're reporting from the air there now, doesn't it, buddy? Now, checking your afternoon weather. . ."

The newspapers in India gave their readers tips on confronting these elephants if they came their way. Tip number one: "Never stand in an elephant's path." (I'm telling the truth.) Tip number two: "Whatever you do, don't try to make eye contact."

Okay.

How would one know an elephant's path, is my question? Is there some sort of pattern wild elephants have when trampling? Maybe this is where algebra would come in handy.

But really, I doubt if the person who would play chicken with an elephant—or attempt staring one down—would be the kind of individual who would read a newspaper. What do you think?

In New York City I'll bet they would yell at the elephants to get their big, fat, long noses out of the stinkin' road before they get shot.

I guess there are no givens anymore. If there ever were any. I still see Americans throw hurricane parties which is about as dumb as trying to stare down an oncoming elephant. How about that CNN reporter who covers hurricanes holding onto a flagpole? Parallel to the ground. How about that guy's mental state? Does Elmore in Louisiana—chompin' on a slab of ribs after a hard day's work—really hear anything he says?

"Hey, Lucy! Come in here, baby! Look at this fool! Whoa! Look at those pants fly, hun! The man's reporting in his drawers, Lucy! The boy's in his Hanes! I thought this was a family show! Take the kids in the other room, baby."

Sometimes I wonder why we need to be told the obvious. Perhaps it's because we all need reminders? "Buckle your seat belts," I say to our family each time we get in our van. I've seen the consequences of not wearing a safety belt.

You know, the Bible has some not-so-dumb tips for a fulfilling life. They're not tips, really—they are commandments for righteous living. Commandments which, if followed, will put us in the center of God's will for our lives.

Two of these are found in Matthew 22:34–40 where the Bible reads, "Hearing that Jesus had silenced the Sadducees, the Pharisees got together. One of them, an expert in the law, tested him with this question: 'Teacher, which is the greatest commandment in the Law?' "

"Jesus replied: 'Love the Lord your God with all your heart and with all your soul and with all your mind. This is the first and greatest commandment. And the second is like it: Love your neighbor as yourself. All the Law and Prophets hang on these two commandments' " (NIV).

You know, most of the time we dig our own holes, don't we? Sure, things out of our control happen and adversely affect our lives. But we suffer often in this life because we refuse to heed God's commandments and abide by His principles. On the one hand, to walk outside God's will is asking for trouble. In a very real and spiritual sense, we're inviting the same kind of trouble one gets when standing in the path of a wild elephant. On the other hand, to follow Jesus Christ, abide by His principles, and live in the center of His will, is to live a life of peace, joy, and contentment.

Now, for those of you traveling to India, remember:

Don't stand in the path of an elephant and never ever try to stare one down. It wouldn't be prudent.

Don't say ol' Tim didn't warn you.

THESE THREE THINGS

1. God's commandments are meant for our well-being, protection, and happiness.

2. Jesus said the greatest commandment in the Scripture is to love God with all our heart, with all our soul, and with all our mind.

3. When confronted with the choice of India or Mexico for the foreign mission field, go with Mexico. Yes, the roads are terrible, but at least there are no wild elephants to contend with.

OFF THE RECORD

"Momma, you'll be proud.
I shared my lunch
with everyone today,
even Jesus."

–Young boy with five loaves
and two fish

FISH FOR THOUGHT

Can you imagine being inside the belly of a whale? I know, you were thinking about that just the other day in the waiting room of the dentist's office in between reading old *Good Housekeeping* magazines, weren't you? I think this particular fish phobia—if you will—was the only subject Phil Donahue didn't get around to in his twenty-five-year talk show career. Honestly, I really don't care to imagine being inside the belly of a whale—or large fish, as the New International Version reads.

First, whales are notorious for poor personal hygiene, and a steady diet of seals and giant squids is known to cause terrible breath. (I saw this on a Jacques Cousteau special once, I think. It may have been Carol Burnett, so don't hold me to it.) Secondly, warm, humid conditions just sap the life right out of you after a while. I know, I'm from the Deep South.

But such was the situation of a man named Jonah. His story can be found between the books of Obadiah and Micah. (No, no. That's Old Testament. You really should read your Bible more so you don't embarrass yourself, always having to look over at your neighbor in Sunday school class to see which direction she's going.)

The first few verses read: "The word of the Lord came to Jonah son of Amittai: Go to the great city of Nineveh and preach against it, because its wickedness has come up before me. But Jonah ran away from the Lord and headed for Tarshish. He went down to Joppa, where he found a ship bound for that port. After paying the fare, he went aboard and sailed for Tarshish to flee from the Lord" (NIV).

As a kid, I loved it when Mom or Dad would read the little Bible storybook—with pictures of course—about Jonah. I could see myself in the belly of a whale. For some reason this fascinated me. I guess it was the idea of a big fish eating a human, like something you might find in a scary movie. I also wondered what Jonah did during the time he was down there. Did he, like, go exploring the bowels of the fish? Did he use the tongue for a water slide? As a child listening to this story, your imagination does run wild.

Now, I don't know about you, but if I were going

to run away from the Lord, I would find some more appealing place to go than a town called Tarshish. Sounds like something New Yorkers put on a hot dog.

God said go, and Jonah said—at least with his actions—no way.

I wonder what was going through Jonah's mind when he decided to "run away" from Almighty God? How does one make travel plans to hide from the Creator of the Universe? Somehow, I think Jonah knew he couldn't physically get away from the Lord. Maybe he thought that if he turned and went the other way the Lord would accept his answer and drop the issue, or call someone else to go tell those folks they were wicked.

Calling people to repentance from sin and wickedness was not the most enjoyable of tasks in those days. Men weren't waiting in line to go speak to the people about the holiness and righteousness of God and His judgment. The same is true today. We need Christian leaders who will issue a clarion call to America that rebellion against God will lead to our own demise.

I'm sure that one of the main reasons Jonah desired to stay away from what God had called him to do in Nineveh was that he didn't want to be the center of controversy. Who needs the criticism? Who needs the heat?

Jesus didn't go looking for trouble and controversy but He met it—in large part—because of what He stood for and stood against. His values. His standards. Yes, His morality. He stood for holiness and righteousness and against sin and wickedness. It seems to me it was when He spoke against sin that He made a lot of people angry. They didn't like being confronted with their sin. The same can be said of Paul, Peter, and many of the other leaders in the early church.

Today God still needs men and women, boys and girls, to speak His truth in love.

Always remember, it is wise to do what the Lord calls us to do, regardless of the unpopularity of the task. And besides, there are worse places to be than preaching in Nineveh. Like the belly of a whale, for instance.

THESE THREE THINGS

1. No matter how we may want to sometimes, like Jonah, we can't hide from God.

2. If the Lord tells us to do something, even things we really don't want to do, it is far better to obey than to ignore Him.

3. Read Captain Cousteau's (or Jacques-my-man, for close friends) classic, *The Personal Hygiene of Whales: The Real Story.*

"Now, where did y'all put
those termites anyway?"

–Noah to his sons

Forever Together?

Alison and I got our invitation in the spring to our ten-year high school reunion later in the summer. We were high school sweethearts and graduated together. She with honors and me—well—I just graduated. I still haven't used algebra. I'm beginning to think I was lied to about this crazy so-called "math" being somehow helpful in life. Other than you engineers, will all those who've actually used algebra since school please raise your hands? Thank you. Just what I thought. I wonder if school administrators are catching on to this? The other day I saw my old junior college algebra professor greeting folks at Wal Mart.

To go or not to go to the reunion? That was our question. We both did and didn't care about going. You know how that is. It would be fun to see all our old classmates and friends, but then, we really didn't think we would have that much in common with many of them. We were conservative in our lifestyle and most of them were not.

After some discussion, Alison and I did go to our class reunion in 1991. Tupelo High School, class of 1981. But it could have been any high school reunion, USA. Lots of people, lots of hugs, lots of smiles and beneath it all, I'm sure, a lot of hurts.

As I got to visit with some of my old friends I was stunned at how many of them were already divorced. Alison and I, married seven years at the time, seemed to be in the minority because we were still together. Near the end of the reunion I began talking to one of my friends who was standing alone and whom I hadn't seen in five years. I made the comment that I couldn't believe how many of our classmates were already divorced. He replied, "Yeah, I've been in and out of it myself since I saw you last."

I sipped on my soft drink, said that I was sorry to hear that, and we started talking about other things. But I began to think even as we talked, *In and out of it?* This "it" you're talking about is holy matrimony. What is going on here? What does this say about my generation? Doesn't anybody ever stay together anymore? What about the marriage vows before God? What about the children?

Michael Martin Murphy sings many songs I

really enjoy. Although I never really understood "Wildfire," it was still a great song. The lyrics are kind of hazy, but it's something about a girl picking up a boy on a horse—named Wildfire—something, something, by the fall of the moon and there was a hoot owl making noises by the boy's window for six nights in a row, something, something, killing frost. Great song, "Wildfire." Martin had another popular tune in the early '90s asking the same questions going through my mind that evening at the reunion: "So what's the glory in living? Doesn't anybody ever stay together anymore? And if love never lasts forever, then what's forever for?"

Now I certainly don't want to sound or be self-righteous. But for the grace of God, there go I. And I know that different circumstances surround each marriage and divorce and sometimes people get married for all the wrong reasons. However, there's no question that the root cause of the divorce epidemic in my generation is sin, in particular the sin of selfishness (something I have to fight every day, so I really have no room for self-righteousness). Selfishness puts one's own needs, wants, and desires above everyone else, including the spouse he or she vowed to "love and to cherish till death do us part." Selfishness leaves little or no room for love, commitment, or responsibility. It scoffs at these values.

If Alison and I were in the minority at our class reunion, the reason is clearly that marriages based on Jesus Christ are in the minority. Jesus says that to serve Him faithfully in my marriage; I am to put my wife before myself in word, deed, and thought. However I fail—and I do fail often—that is the standard by which I must be judged by God and man. True happiness and contentment come when I fulfill that commandment to serve Him first by putting myself last.

By the way, during the day we were all asked—about two hundred of us—to vote for the most changed male and female. Keep in mind when I graduated from high school I was five-ten, 138 pounds, had shoulder-length hair, and wasn't really one to stand up in a crowd and do the right thing. Sometimes I liked being the life of the party and I'm not talkin' Sunday school parties.

At the reunion I was five-ten, 180 pounds, receding hairline, and I didn't mind telling people that no, I didn't want a beer, and yes, I was a Christian, I still loved Alison with all my heart and, yes, I knew she was the best-looking woman in the crowd. (She's also the best wife and mother in the whole bunch.) And to top it off, I was looking forward to being a tied-down husband and father for the next twenty years (or more).

Any more questions?

Well, for whatever reasons, I won the Most Changed Award that summer's night. I walked up to receive whatever it was they gave me as the disc jockey played "In the Long Run," by the Eagles. Maybe it was the weight and hair. But I like to think it was—however flawed it may have been—a small witness to the grace of God and the life-changing power of Jesus Christ.

The song was kind of fitting, don't you think? It's got a great beat too. Sing it with me. Sing it out loud.

". . .I know we can make it, if our love is a strong one. . .in the long. . .ooooh, long run. . ."

Hey, where are you going? Don't turn the page now, this is good stuff. . .hey, come back. . .

THESE THREE THINGS

1. Selfishness can kill good relationships. In marriage, we should try to outserve one another.

2. Jesus Christ is the life-changer and the bond that can hold marriages together.

3. I know I can't sing a lick and the Eagles should probably sue me to keep me from ever singing one of their songs in a book again.

"Excuse me.
Anyone seen a bunch of pigs
wandering around here anywhere?
I went off to answer nature's call
for a few minutes and
now I can't find 'em. . ."

–Pig owner after Jesus casts
the demons into the swine

ARMPIT ROBBERY

Pet stealing is rare, I think. Ace Ventura is the only pet detective I've heard of. And he's a fictional character in one of Jim Carey's wacko movies. But Ace—or his real-life counterpart, if there is such a professional—was almost needed in Seaside, Oregon, when a crustacean became the target of theft. That's right, a crustacean.

I like saying that word, don't you? Crustacean. Feels good just rolling off your tongue. Say it again. Cruuuuuuuuuuuustacean.

Anyway, the following appeared in newspapers recently:

Victor the twenty-five-pound lobster has been rescued once again.

The prize crustacean avoided a dunking in boiling water when an alert staffer at Seaside Aquarium foiled the lobster-napping.

Becky Bierly was taking tickets when the abduction began. "She noticed a guy who had come in earlier walking out with our twenty-five-pound lobster under his arm," aquarium manager Keith Chandler said.

Bierly called Chandler, who gave chase. Despite the Labor Day crowds thronging the oceanfront, Chandler quickly located Victor and the alleged abductor.

Here, readers, we have the process of elimination working quite well.

When Chandler confronted the man, he dropped the lobster and walked away.

Chandler took Victor back to his tank, and police arrested Terry Lutz, 35, of Estaceda, on theft charge.

Terry, Terry, Terry. What are we going to do with you, son?

I know the journalist who wrote the above was taught to use the word "alleged" until the "suspect" is found guilty of criminal charges. But really, either you have a twenty-five-pound lobster under your arm or you don't. There's no gray area here.

What could Terry have possibly said to Mr. Chandler and the security in his defense if he were trying to play innocent? He might have said something like this when confronted.

"Well, unbelievable! Would you look at this? A huge lobster has done crawled up my leg and lodged itself under my armpit and I didn't even know it! I'm so sorry, sir, I'll bet you want it back, don't you? I don't know how this could have happened."

Looking down at his two kids—in classic Chevy Chase Vacation movie fashion—he says, "You kids. I'll tell you, officer, these kids of mine are always playing practical jokes on me and I've told them, one day these little pranks are going to get us all in trouble. And a lobster for goodness sakes! We've been over the evils of lobster theft time and time again. Stay away from drugs, say no to strangers, and by all means, don't steal other people's lobsters. I don't know what we're going to do, officer. I honestly don't. Sometimes you just want to throw your arms up in the air and give up. You've got kids don't you, officer? You know what I mean."

Seriously, lying, cheating, and stealing is becoming the norm for us Americans. I ran across a survey recently which stunned me. It was in *USA Weekend*, which is a weekend supplement to newspapers much like *Parade*. It read:

Who hasn't read the headlines or watched the network newscasts without a sinking heart and a sense of loss? Teens jailed on drug charges. Teen indicted for cheating on SAT. Whatever happened to yesterday's moral dilemmas—whether it was OK to cut class for a baseball game or to smoke a cigarette behind the garage? Do today's teens know right from wrong?

The answer is maybe not. A write-in survey by *USA Weekend* of an estimated 126,000 kids, ages 13–18, shows that 25–40 percent of teens see nothing wrong with cheating on exams, stealing from employers, or keeping money that isn't theirs.

Wow! Think about that for a minute. The dominant philosophy of moral relativism America has embraced the last twenty-five years is certainly filtering down. These numbers must change if we are to carry any semblance of a civilized society into the twenty-first century. It is up to Christians to hold up the standard of righteousness and objective truth as found in the Holy Bible. No one else will. As Ted Koppel once said speaking to a group of graduates at Duke University, "What Moses brought down from the mountain was not the ten suggestions."

God's moral laws, such as the Ten Commandments and the Sermon on the Mount, never change.

These laws and principles transcend people, transcend cultures, and transcend time. Jesus said in Matthew 24:35, "Heaven and earth will pass away, but my words will never pass away" (NIV). By the way, I don't know whatever happened to our lobster thief, Terry. My guess is he opened a seafood restaurant called Lobsters-R-Us somewhere in Oregon.

THESE THREE THINGS

1. To better understand how moral relativism has gotten a death grip on America, read Charles Colson's book *Against the Night*.

2. God's instructions for moral and righteous living are found in the Scriptures and are forever fixed.

3. Twenty-five-pound crustaceans are near impossible to hide under one's arm. (Kids, don't try this at home without parental supervision.)

OFF THE RECORD

"You guys go ahead.
My horse has a
cramp or something."

–One Egyptian solider after seeing
the Red Sea parted

OF FATHERS AND CHILDREN

I have always been interested in the parallel between the parent-child relationship and God's relationship with us, His children. I became increasingly aware of how the Lord may see us sometimes when my first child, Wriley Hope, turned two years old.

Long before she had reached that age, Alison and I decided that we would refer to this one year in Wriley's life as the "terrific twos." All we had ever heard about was the "terrible twos" and we in our inexperience and ignorance thought that the twos couldn't be that big a deal. However, we have since recanted the "terrific twos" statement and realized how very naive we were to expect the twos to be terrific. There's a reason the term "terrible twos" has been around since little Cain and Abel roamed the earth. And positive thinking can only deal with so much reality until it cries uncle.

This all came home to me after a five-minute experience in the convenience store with Wriley. I must say that I suspect my daughter was atypical. Whereas the normally aggressive child is a type A personality, Wriley Hope was an AAA. Like that irritating little bunny on the battery commercial that makes us all want to shoot our television sets, she kept going, and going, and going. And then going some more. She's changed some since then, praise be to God, but at the time Alison and I considered having her tested for whatever it is they test children for who behave as she did. Maybe she had Attention Shoppers Disorder or whatever they call it? We didn't know what to call it besides, "Wriley, bad girl." That seemed kind of simplistic to me (I'm a redneck, yes, but one of depth and sophistication). We needed something more clinical sounding, I told Alison many times. (This was 1989, before half the nation came down with Attention Deficit Disorder.)

One evening, the whole family drove to the convenience store, and Wriley in a half-asking, half-demanding sort of way let it be known that she wanted to go in the store with me. *No problem*, I thought. Quick in, quick out. We made our way through the door and toward the aisle to get some baby food for her nine-month-old brother Wesley. Wriley held my hand sweetly and behaved very well until she saw what I call Candy Row. This area of the store has a magnetic pull on children. With all its vibrant color, the candy wrapping is most appealing to the eye and, with all the sugar, the contents inside the wrapping are most appealing to the taste buds of most folks. Especially small children.

Immediately, upon seeing Sugar City, she shook my hand loose and went to the candy. (At this point, I discovered that it is futile to try to talk with a child about the lust of the flesh or self-control.) *Let her look, what's the harm?* I thought. I also quickly reasoned that I could go ahead and get the baby food and dash back to Wriley before any real damage was done. I was only one row over, after all.

"Okay, let's see here, banana food jar, banana food jar, where's b-a-n-a-n-a? . . . Banana, banana, banana, where is the stupid banana jar?" I said to myself. "Okay, find the banana jar, Tim! Come on, buddy. For once, go in a store, and come through for your family, son." (Sometimes, I take on the duel roles of father and son when I'm in a testosterone-testing situation such as this.) Alison—who was waiting in the car with Wesley—had told me specifically, twice, to get banana food. She even looked me in the eye just before I closed the door—as she often does—and said, "B-A-N-A-N-A, Tim. It's not hard."

"It's not here," I thought aloud in frustration. "I'm looking directly at the fruit section, and it's not anywhere in sight. We've got your apricot, pineapple, peach, every kind of fruit known to man including gordash—what's gordash?—but this is my luck, there's no b-a-n-a-n-a here."

I almost grabbed two other customers by the arm as they came down the aisle. "Excuse me, do you see any banana food on this shelf anywhere? Five bucks says you can't find any. Go ahead, look. No really, I've got Abe Lincoln right here."

Why me? Why here? Why now? I thought. As soon as I go out to the car and tell Al there's no b-a-n-a-n-a, she'll walk right in here, whereupon the evil and scheming little beady-eyed clerk will have quickly placed several banana jars on the shelf and Alison will find them and she'll give me that "once again you're not paying attention look," sigh, and walk to the counter holding Wesley in one arm, Wriley by the hand, and her purse in her secret third arm (I swear she's got four). Then she'll tell me to go get in the car in front of several other men, I'll go out to the car, pull on the door handle twice, only to remember she has the keys to the locked car. But I don't dare go back in. I'll just stand there by my car door, say "how you doin'" and "nice to see ya" to the folks that walk by and look stupid. For those scoring at home, we have shot par here, ladies and gentlemen.

That, my friends, is a lot to think about. Which is probably why I couldn't find the b-a-n-a-n-a fruit jar in the first place. All this stress is too much for an American male trying to keep up with who's going to win the National League's Eastern division. But I'm not one to make excuses. Very often anyway.

Now, the moment of truth. Do I continue to search for the banana baby food, or do I go around the corner and get Wriley? The pressure mounted, the sweat beads began to form on my temples. I couldn't just pick up any old jar with some flavor that would probably cause Wesley to cry all night! I began to hear the closing notes from Jeopardy. (So, I'm exaggerating the drama a bit here. Work with me.) However, I decided, in haste I suppose, because there seemed no time for prayer or counsel, to scrap my search for the bananas, grab the mixed fruits jar—which was pretty close to bananas in my book—and retrieve Wriley. Yes, food for the children is important, but you've got to keep the children around first. It's called priorities, but that's another story.

It's fruity decisions like these that make a man what he is. I'm not sure exactly what that means, but I think Winston Churchill or C.S. Lewis said it, so it means something really important, I'm sure.

Decision made, I rounded the corner to catch a glimpse of Wriley sprinting toward the checkout counter, ripping paper from candy as she ran. All of this was, of course, enjoyed by an amused audience of customers and a smiling clerk. When it's not their child, people are amused. Her intent was to get the candy into her mouth before I could say no or ask her to give it to me. She almost succeeded, but I intercepted her hand just short of her open mouth. I then reasoned with her—as best one can reason with a two-year-old—that we must pay for the candy before eating it. Larry Burkett stuff.

I then decided to hold the child firmly—but gently, of course—while I secured the other item I needed. She quickly squirmed out of my arms, and headed for a "hun bun," as she called her favorite breakfast food and one of the five major food groups of two-years-olds. (The others being peppermint sticks, Fruit Loops, french fries, and bubble gum.) She began smashing the pastry with her hands. We've all seen children do this, haven't we? Just mush and squash a fresh, new pastry for no apparent reason. Calling her name no less than five times (something I tend to do when anger erupts), I stopped her from completely destroying the "hun bun" and held her hand (gently, but firmly) as we made our way back to the checkout counter.

Almost home free, I thought, so I released her hand and told her to stand right beside me while I paid. As the clerk was ringing up my bill, I heard the distinctive sound of plastic objects crashing to the ground right behind me. Cringing, I turned, only to discover that my wife's daughter had leveled to the floor what had once been a tall, orderly pyramid of twenty soft drink bottles.

Now I'm not trying to excuse Wriley, but why do stores do this? What real purpose does it serve to stack cola bottles up where the slightest movement can cause bottles to fall all over the place? I've surveyed seventy-three store managers and have not had one answer that made any sense. I encourage you to do your own survey and see if you don't get the same results.

As the clerk handed me my change, I became acutely aware—by virtue of the fact that my leg was experiencing a wet, sticky sensation—that one of the bottles was spewing all over the store. The cola was spraying everywhere. People were jumping around like kangaroos. I also noticed the friendly clerk was no longer smiling. I grabbed the spewing bottle and sheepishly handed it to the clerk as customers continued to scatter out of harm's way. As the clerk made her way to the back with the bottle—mumbling under her breath—I hurried from the store, daughter in tow.

A few days later, certainly not that night, I reflected rationally on that experience and wondered how often it is that I behave in front of God, my Heavenly Father, the way Wriley behaved in front of me that evening. How often do I run for "candy row" and dart off in my own direction when God would have me walk with Him? And when I "escape" from God's will, all too often I find myself knocking over the bottles; it is then that God takes me (gently, but firmly) by the hand and leads me back onto the right path, the path of obedience.

As patient and loving as I am with my daughter as she grows, matures, and yes, bridles her passions, it's a comfort to know that my Heavenly Father is infinitely more patient and loving with me.

THESE THREE THINGS

1   Just like Wriley ran from me, enthralled
    by the world around her, we can make a
    mess of our lives if we run away from
    God.

2. A parent must teach a child to bridle his
    passions for his own protection, just as
    God's Holy Spirit leads us to bridle ours
    for the same.

3. Store managers who stack pyramids of
    plastic bottled colas deserve what they
    get. (Gordash is not a fruit. Or a
    vegetable. Or a barnyard animal. Or
    anything on earth that I know of. Ha!
    Ha! Had you wondering there for a
    minute, didn't I?)

OFF THE RECORD

"No, no, it's not luck, Andrew.
It's called providential fishing."

–Peter one day on the
Sea of Galilee

ALVIN AND HENRY

Determination and devotion are good qualities to have, Dad always said. You know, the "where there is a will, there is a way" philosophy. "You can do anything you set your mind to," Dad told me my first year of college. That was the problem. I was putting my mind on poker games four nights a week and was getting pretty good at it. It was a lot more fun than going to class.

But it was the school part that pained me first. Then it pained my dad when he got my grades. Then, in turn, Dad pained me again. We spent the year feeling each other's pain. It was a vicious cycle.

While it's a good character trait most of the time, determination can also be misguided. Determination to do what, one must ask? Then there is the "determination" gray area. An example of this is found in the story below involving one Alvin Straight of Blue River, Wisconsin:

Blue River, Wisconsin—No driver's license? No problem for seventy-three-year-old Alvin Straight. He recently completed a six-week 240-mile trek on his riding lawnmower from his home in Laurens in northeastern Iowa to visit his brother in southwestern Wisconsin.

Neither brother can see well enough to get a driver's license, but neither wants to let someone else drive.

Just like a man, isn't it? I think it's a safe bet Alvin didn't ask for directions either. The article continued:

When Straight learned that his eighty-year-old brother, Henry, suffered a stroke, he knew he had to visit. He bought a 1966 John Deere lawn mower, got a ten-foot trailer to haul gasoline, clothes, food, and camping equipment and took off. Was he worried about his safety?

"What would I be scared of? I went through combat in World War II. They ain't going to show me a thing I haven't seen before," Straight said. "I've got two good canes."

Henry didn't know his brother was coming.

Now wouldn't you have liked to listen in on the conversation the two highway patrolmen had as they pulled up beside Alvin?

"Hey, Joe, what do you make of this?"

"I don't know, pull over and let's see how far this guy's going. Tough-looking old codger. It's five miles 'till the next exit."

After talking with my man Alvin, Joe walks back to the patrol car and bends into the driver's window.

"Says, ah, says he's ah. . ."

"Well?"

I don't know about you but I've got Alvin dressed up in an old army jacket, with goggles and a scarf blowing in the wind. Sort of like Snoopy. I guess what makes this story so interesting to me is that Alvin's actions represent the best and worst of human nature simultaneously.

Alvin's actions demonstrated commitment, care, and love, while at the same time demonstrating extreme pride, stubbornness, and, well, shall we say, lack of good judgment. And that's being very kind to Alvin.

Don't you wonder what kind of message Alvin left on his answering machine?

"Hello, this here's Alvin Straight. I'll be out on the road for a couple of months going to see my brother. If that's you, Pete, calling to complain about my lawn, save it. I'll bush-hog it when I get back. Why don't you just mind your own business anyway. For others, please leave a message after the reveille finishes playing. Thank you."

I don't know exactly what kind of lesson we can learn from Alvin. He did have good intentions at heart. There's no question about that. You have to say he does love his brother.

Despite what I think about the sanity of doing what Alvin did, it kind of reminds me of the story in the Bible Jesus gave us about the good shepherd who left the hundred sheep and went looking for the one lost lamb (Luke 15:4).

Like Alvin was to his brother, the good shepherd was devoted to that little lost lamb. He cared deeply about the welfare of that one lost lamb. In the same way, our Heavenly Father is devoted to us if we will only heed His call to come to His open arms. He is the Good Shepherd. The attitude of the good shepherd in the parable Jesus told was, "Whatever it takes."

I have to ask myself, am I as devoted, as committed, as determined in my relationships with Alison, the kids, the cause of Christ? Do I go the extra mile? Or in Alvin's case, the extra 240 miles?

But, Al, the next time you make the 240-mile journey on your lawn mower, please call ahead, buddy. Henry had no idea you were coming and, well, he went to Florida on vacation.

Just kiddin' folks. Alvin and Henry did get together. And no, I don't know how Alvin got home. I don't really want to know.

THESE THREE THINGS

1. Jesus Christ went the extra mile—the road to Calvary—for you and me to set us free.

2. Alvin's demonstration of love overcomes the craziness of his idea. Barely.

3. Always call ahead when you're going to ride 240 miles on a lawn mower to make sure your party will actually be there when you arrive.

OFF THE RECORD

"Tell me,
is revenge really sweet?"

–Joseph to a friend

NOT FOR HUMAN
CONSUMPTION

One hot and humid summer afternoon—there's no other kind in the Deep South—just before Independence Day weekend a couple of years back, my father-in-law Jim and I took my two oldest children fishing. Wriley, my then six-year-old daughter, and Wesley, my five-year-old son, went with us to a catfish pond, the kind where you pay for the fish you catch.

You sort of feel like you're cheating, since you know the pond is stocked with catfish, but it's still fun to see the look in the kids' eyes when the fish takes the bait and the fluorescent bobber goes under water. And if you can't catch fish here, well, you might as well take up knitting.

Anyway, on this sticky July day, after having minor success with rooster liver for bait, my father-in-law pulled from the cooler a plastic container of "Big Bite Catfish Dough." Big Bite is made in Edmond, Oklahoma. Says so in bold type on the container.

One of the places I want to visit now that Charles Kuralt has retired to that great RV in the sky and I'll likely be taking his place, is Edmond, Oklahoma. Why? So I can go see where and how they make Big Bite Catfish Dough. Just what is their secret recipe? I consider it a part of my American heritage— at least my Southern heritage—to see it for myself. Maybe I can talk Alison into making it a Great American Family Vacation at Catfishland. Well, on second thought, maybe not. She really likes the beach.

Now for those who aren't familiar with catfish dough, let's just say catfish are attracted by odor. And not necessarily pleasant odor. In fact, catfish dough stinks, and it looks as bad as it smells. But then again, it's made to stink. (And, not that I really wanted to know, but the ingredients are not listed on the side.) Believe me, to the average human there is absolutely nothing appealing about catfish dough.

But on the side of that container—and I am telling the truth here—in big, bold, black print were printed the words: "NOT FOR HUMAN CONSUMPTION." I kid you not. And we're not talking fine print here, we're talking big, bold, black print on a white container: "NOT FOR HUMAN CONSUMPTION."

Now, I'm wondering. I know Americans are a diverse lot, and walking among us are a lot of strange people with peculiar tastes (no pun intended), but as I asked my father-in-law upon reading this, "When did this become a problem? Have I missed a special report on CNN?"

Bernard Shaw here with a late-breaking story. Today the president—in a historic move—ordered the Food and Drug Administration to immediately begin making sure all catfish dough companies do a more thorough job of preventing people from eating their product.

It seems many Americans—and we won't mention what region of the country they live in—are buying catfish dough, instead of the always popular deviled ham, to spread on sandwiches. CNN White House sources say the president will address this national health crisis in the State of the Union address and will make a plea that this practice stop as it is a bad example for the children of America. For the record, the president said he once sniffed catfish dough in college, but that he never actually ingested the substance.

Talk about new fodder for Jeff Foxworthy!

Are insurance companies refusing to pay for hospital treatment for those who consume catfish dough? You couldn't blame them.

"I'm sorry, I must have misunderstood you, Mr. Johnson. You had to be hospitalized for eating what?"

Now I can imagine someone writing the Big Bite company a letter: Dear Big Bite, I'm not one to be critical, but after using your dough I must say Pillsbury has got ya beat hands down. And furthermore, I didn't taste any of the catfish flavor I was 'specting with the big catfish on the front of the can and all. Talk about false advertising. Now if you want to give me a year's supply free I might consider coming back. Sincerely, Dixie Dan.

Well, I'm having a lot of fun with this, but really, the experience caused me to wonder about matters of spiritual consumption. Can our soul's health and well-being be affected by what we consume? I think so. When we obsess on the negative things of life, it's as though we are gobbling up smelly catfish bait—and yet we often do just that.

A quick look at the book of Ephesians tells us a few other things that are not fit for human consumption, all of which can make us spiritually ill if allowed to be a part of our life. In fact, chapter four, verses 29–32 reads: "Do not let any unwholesome talk come out of your mouths, but only what is helpful for building others up, according to their needs, that it may benefit those who listen. And do not grieve the Holy Spirit of God, with whom you were sealed for the day of redemption. Get rid of all bitterness, rage and anger, brawling and slander, along with every form of malice. Be kind and compassionate to one another, forgiving each other, just as in Christ God forgave you."

God's Word should be our guide as to what is good and what is not when it comes to what we allow into our hearts, minds, and spirits.

Now as for the stomach, I have to think that even the Lord shakes His head when one of His children partakes of Big Bite catfish bait.

THESE THREE THINGS

1. Followers of Jesus need to consume the Word of God on a regular basis.

2. Bitterness, anger, rage, and unwholesome talk are poisonous to the soul the same way catfish dough is sickening to the stomach. They're not for human consumption.

3. Despite what some are saying, catfish dough does not taste like. . .chicken. (This is strictly an assumption.)

"You're up first.
This better be good."

–Mark, Luke, and John
to Matthew

It's a Wonderful Life?

Like most Christians, I've heard the four spiritual laws used by Campus Crusade for Christ for years. I've even used the Four Spiritual Laws leaflet in sharing my faith. But I always wondered if there didn't need to be a qualifier on the first one. "God loves you, and offers a wonderful plan for your life," it reads.

So what if I get run over by a truck when I walk out of this church? Is that a "wonderful" plan for my life? What if I find out next week I've got terminal cancer? Is that a "wonderful" plan for my life? What if I get home to find my neighbor's dog has dug up the flower bed I worked all summer to perfect? Is that a "wonderful" plan for my life? Okay, so forget the dog problem, what about the other two?

In fact, does God really have a plan for my life at

all? If so, how do I know it's wonderful? Or is this just a bunch of 1990s, feel-good Christian-speak we've adapted from Tony Robbins so those who wouldn't otherwise listen to sin, death, and hell will tune us in? Who defines "wonderful"? These are some very legitimate questions that deserve real, straightforward answers.

When I was a kid growing up I got the question like all kids do, "Whatcha gonna be when you grow up?" Adults like to do this to see what kind of answers they get from the little people. Then they chuckle and rub your head. It's also a standard grown-up question when they're not in the mood to be original or when they don't have anything better to ask. Then they chuckle and rub your head.

Like a lot of other kids, especially boys, when I was ten and eleven I wanted to be a professional athlete. I was convinced this was God's wonderful plan for my life. Back then guys like Pete Rose, "Pistol" Pete Maravich, and Roger Staubauch were popular. It didn't really matter to me, football, basket-ball, or baseball. I could see myself making them all. I could have been the Dieon Sanders or Bo Jackson of my day if not for a few obstacles fate threw my way.

When I was twelve I learned that I couldn't stay in the batter's box for a curveball. In baseball, this weeds out the sissies from the good players real quick. I was a sissy. For those of you who've never experienced a curveball, it's like this. The pitcher—in my case it was Peter West, who is now my dentist—throws the ball fast and hard. The ball looks like it's going to crack your skull or cause disfigurement, so naturally you jump back six feet, hit the dirt, and get out of the ball's flight pattern. Sometimes the ball doesn't have a pattern. This will cause the strong emotion of fear to rear its ugly head. (It's a healthy fear, though. A God-given survival instinct, it is.) The ball then—theoretically—"curves" back over the plate, the umpire calls a strike, you get up visibly shaken, get back in the batter's box, and do the same thing over again. It takes three of these before you can say "Thank You, God" and go back to the dugout. Panic-stricken.

But the hardest part is acting as if you're angry at yourself for striking out as you head back to the dugout. You've got to play this little game if you want to maintain any respect from your dad, coach, or teammates. It's typical macho stuff. Banging yourself on the head, slamming the bat on the ground kind of stuff. But on the inside, you're just happy to be alive and breathing and you pray you don't have to face Peter West again.

That's why I didn't make the major leagues.

As for football, it was the first day of practice in ninth grade. It was August in Mississippi—100 degrees and the air thick as molasses—and the coach made us run a couple of miles. While running around the practice field sucking air, I noticed that most of the other guys had been working out with weights and were much, much bigger and stronger than was I. A quick mental deduction told me that if my 120 pounds of skin and bone collided with any one of the many 200-pound masses of muscle and granite, I would likely die. At the very least it would be an extremely painful experience and I wasn't into pain. I didn't come back for day two. I quit, and that's why I'm here today.

It is obvious to me now that it was not God's wonderful plan for my life that I be a professional athlete. If it were, He would have given me a bigger, stronger, faster, quicker body, and the fearlessness to stay in the batter's box for Peter's curveball. So, not playing left field and batting cleanup for the St. Louis Cardinals, how do I know I am in God's will today?

Good question. You're a very perceptive reader. Answer: Fundamentally, I believe God's will for me— or any of His children—is to obey His word, which is the Holy Bible. No matter what happens and where you are in life, trust and obey. Simple answer? Yes.

Easy to follow? No.

If I'm being obedient to the Word of God, then I am in His will. Yes, there are issues of major significance in our lives about which we should seek wise and godly counsel. Marriage and career decisions for instance. However, 95 percent of our time, I believe the Lord's will is clear. That according to the latest *USA Today*/CNN/Gallop poll. Wait a minute. I'm sorry, wrong survey. Too much CNN. That should be according to the Father/Son/Holy Spirit survey—the one that really counts and has a 0.00 percent margin of error. Survey says: Read the Bible, study the Bible, and live the life principles found therein.

So then if we define "wonderful" as the Bible does in John 10:10 as meaningful and purposeful, then it doesn't really matter if I get run over by a truck ten minutes after hearing and believing God has a wonderful plan for my life. For a lot of folks, that shocks the system. But either it's true, or the "wonderful" life promise is not true and should be dropped from our spiritual repertoire. (Repertoire: baseball term used to describe the various pitches guys like Peter West can use against sissies like me.)

"And the world is passing away, and the lust of it; but he who does the will of God abides forever," says 1 John 2:17 (NKJV).

Yes, I want to live a long, healthy, productive life here on earth. Who doesn't? But really, in the final analysis, abiding in Christ—here, now, and forever—is indeed, by definition, a wonderful life.

By the way, did I mention that you are a very perceptive reader?

THESE THREE THINGS

1. A wonderful life is defined as knowing
   Jesus Christ and obeying God's Word.

2. Our plans and God's will are not
   necessarily one and the same.

3. Yes, I admit it, I did attempt to manipu-
   late you with flattery when I called you a
   "very perceptive reader" hoping you would
   buy ten copies of this book for your
   friends.

OFF THE RECORD

"Say Sarah,
I know you're going
to think I'm nuts,
but God told me to tell you. . ."

–Abraham, 99, to his wife

CALLED TO COMPASSION

In our town of Tupelo, Mississippi, there is a hot-sandwich place that Alison and I like to frequent. It's a simple place with good food and good prices. A couple of years back we—Alison, I, our six-year-old daughter, Wriley, our four-year-old son, Wesley, and our newborn son, Walker—went in and I seated the kids while Alison ordered the food.

Alison always volunteers to order the food while I seat the children. I finally figured out that these are among her most cherished moments of peace—just waiting in line. No children grabbing her leg or screaming, "Mommy!" just quietly reflecting on the important things of the day like, "Do I want cheese on that burger or not?"

On this particular day the children and I sat down a few tables away from another family. This family of five included one young girl—about fifteen years old,

I guess—who was obviously mentally handicapped. She chewed her food with her mouth wide open, some of it falling out. Her hands went here and there. She stared straight ahead and seemed almost oblivious to those around her, even the older woman—perhaps her mom—who was helping her and calling her name.

I was really hoping Wriley and Wesley wouldn't notice and thus I wouldn't have to explain what was wrong and answer all their questions. As I got the baby situated I noticed Wriley had begun intently watching the young girl and her mother, every few seconds glancing back at me, and I knew the questions were racing through her little mind. She then asked, "Daddy, what's wrong with that girl? She's spitting her food back out of her mouth."

I had known this day would come. And there will be many more the next few years. Days when you try to explain to your children—who think you have all the answers—why life isn't fair and why bad things happen to good people. I wanted to offer her a four-part tape series by Dr. Dobson. But I knew it was just Wriley and me. Me, Mr. Wisdom.

What Wriley didn't know at the time was that when she was born November 3, 1987, in emergency C-section, our doctors thought she might have suffered some brain damage due to asphyxiation. I remember vividly our pediatrician Dr. Gordon Meador coming into our room a few hours after birth with the news that he was requesting a helicopter from University Hospital in Jackson to fly up and transport our little newborn daughter to the neonatology unit where she could be tested and receive more specific medical attention. In addition to her potential brain damage, her kidneys weren't working. This was life-threatening.

We prayed. Many others prayed. Alison's mom went on ahead of us and spent the day praying Scriptures over Wriley. The three-hour drive Alison and I made from Tupelo to Jackson down the Natchez Trace Parkway seemed like three days. Even though we had a peace, I still wondered, *Why is this happening to us?* As much as we say we trust God, don't we all share that thought sometime in our life?

We were told upon arrival that it might be weeks before we could take our firstborn home and she might have suffered some brain damage. We continued to pray. Miraculously, Wriley began to improve by the hour. After some more tests the next day we learned she was a perfectly healthy little girl—all her motor skills looked normal—who had more or less been in a state of shock because of the traumatic circumstances of her birth. Praise God! Within a week, we were headed home.

But the young girl Wriley was watching had a different story to tell. For reasons only God knows, she was afflicted and it looked permanent. *Lord, help her,* I thought.

On this earth, the Lord doesn't right every wrong, I've learned. Sometimes He calms the storm, and other times, He calms His child, the song says. How simple yet how profound. His grace is sufficient.

"Don't stare at those people, sweetheart, it's not nice to stare," I said. "Wriley, some people are born with problems that make it hard for them to do things that other people can do. We need to be extra nice to people like that girl so that she won't feel sad or feel like she doesn't have any friends. Jesus loves that little girl just like He loves you and me. Okay?"

"Okay," she said quietly. "But why is she spitting her food out like that? Can't she eat right, Daddy?"

"No, she has to have people help her eat, go places, and other things," I said. "She needs special care." I wanted to teach my daughter about compassion.

Compassion is, of course, from God. There has never been—nor will there ever be—a more giving and compassionate person than Jesus Christ. This world is bitter, cold, and crusty. A lot of times this writer is bitter, cold, and crusty. I'm not intentional about it, but selfishness and greed tend to nullify compassion in my life. It's a struggle to keep selfishness in check.

I do not have the answers for why this little girl was so afflicted, except the fact that we live in an imperfect and fallen world. But I do know the nature of God is one of compassion. He loves that little girl just as much as He does a Rhodes scholar. Each human life is equally valuable to our loving Heavenly Father.

My dad used to say that God cares as much about the ditchdigger as He does about the President of the United States. It's true.

Nehemiah 9:17 reads: "But you are a forgiving God, gracious and compassionate, slow to anger and abounding in love" (NIV). And I do know the nature of Christ is to have pity. According to Matthew 9:36: "When he [Jesus] saw the crowds, he had compassion on them, because they were harassed and helpless, like sheep without a shepherd" (NIV). And I do know that it should be the nature of believers in Christ to be tender and compassionate, for in Colossians 3:12 Paul writes, "Therefore, as God's chosen people, holy and dearly loved, clothe yourselves with compassion, kindness, humility, gentleness and patience" (NIV).

Well, I suppose the mother of that little girl must have asked the question "Why?" many, many times.

Even so, she was still there extending tender loving care to that little girl, her child. I hope I was able to convey the value of compassion to Wriley. God, help me. We have too many bitter, cold, and crusty people in the world as it is.

THESE THREE THINGS

1. Followers of Jesus Christ are called to compassion, love, and charity.

2. Pray for someone you know who is a caretaker of a mentally or physically disabled person.

3. Lines in fast-food restaurants can actually serve as refuges for beleaguered moms, if but for a few short minutes.

"Dad, it's the cockroaches.
Yes or no?"

–Noah's son as last animals
boarded the ark

BROWNIE POINTS

Determination. Drive. Passion. In their proper context, all describe the manner in which a Christian should live his or her faith. You want to hear about ambition and zeal? The kind that would make Zig Ziglar break down in tears of joy? Check out the following story:

PEORIA, Ariz.—With the slight tilt of her head Sonya Pursehouse says in a singsong voice: "Would you like to buy a box of Girl Scout cookies?"

It must be the dimple in her right cheek.

The eight-year-old doesn't badger people when they say "no," she just turns her sweet smile on the next passerby.

It works. Sonya sold 3,500 boxes of Girl Scout cookies this year, an Arizona record.

She also sold the previous record of 2,300 boxes.

And when she was just six, she sold 1,602 boxes.

"I think she tries to do the best in whatever it is she does," said her father, Tom Pursehouse.

Father and daughter canvassed their neighborhood together. Some days they staked out grocery stores from 8 A.M. until 8 P.M. Once they sold more than 400 boxes in one day.

Wow! I am completely exhausted just thinking about it. On the one hand, I hope my daughter Wriley is like Sonya, and on the other hand, I pray that she isn't.

"Honey, don't you think you're carrying this cookie-selling thing just a little too far? I mean, at last week's meeting we had everyone raise their hands and there wasn't a Brownie in Arizona within 3,000 boxes of you. I think we can go back to six hours of sleep now."

But if Wriley demonstrates such drive, ambition, or craziness—depending on your perspective—it won't be from my genes, I'll tell you that. Perhaps her mom's, but not mine.

I tried this "door-to-door" sales approach a couple of times when I was a kid. I just could not handle the rejection. And this was the early '70s, before everyone got so short, rude, and heartless. Just when Ted

Turner was starting to build his empire, that's when my entrepreneurial spirit was crushed.

I remember when I was ten ordering some Christmas greeting cards—about $25 worth for demonstration—and going around my neighborhood, Lee Acres, in Tupelo knocking on doors. If I knock, they will buy, was my thinking. The year was 1973 and I was fired up at the prospect of making $100 or more which would become my Own Personal Stash. *This is my ticket to all the Butter Fingers, cokes, and comic books I could ever want,* I thought. This is what life is all about. No more asking or begging Mom for money. (Dad rarely had any. Or so he said.) Visions of grandeur raced through my mind. Maybe I'll build a tree house out back, retire, and listen to Cardinal baseball games for the rest of my life. Better yet, maybe I'll move to St. Louis—buy a tree house—and hang out with Bob Gibson, Lou Brock, and the guys. Maybe I'll. . .

No, no, no, no, no, no, no.

Well, maybe not.

I felt good anytime I could get a polite "no, thanks." But it was dejection and rejection city. It really was. And ten-year-olds don't have a Plan B. It got so bad right towards the end that when the people would come to the door I would say something like, "I'm sorry to bother you, I really am, and I know you're not going to be interested in what I have to show you, so why don't I just go ahead and leave. Thank you for your time, ma'am, and may I mow your yard for free for a year or something to make up for my being so inconsiderate and interrupting whatever it was you were doing? Maybe you would like to throw something at me or beat me with that salad spoon or whatever."

But seriously—3,500 Girl Scout cookies sold by one little Brownie in Arizona!

Now, understand, with the Girl Scouts, selling the cookies is just half of the annual project. If you sell them, you *deliver* them. This would be a major crisis in our family, because I'm not renting a U-Haul for three weeks to deliver cookies. I'm just not going to do it. Especially, in 115 degree Arizona heat. In the words of former President George Bush, "It wouldn't be prudent."

When I read about little Sonya, I couldn't help but admire her attitude and determination. And surely she has been rejected hundreds of times. As you could see by my little experience, I gave way to rejection. Sonya's story reminds me also of an experience Paul and Barnabas had in Acts 13. If any man ever lived a passionate life for Jesus Christ, it was Paul.

The Scripture says in verses 44–52 that the two apostles were bold in the face of a hostile group of unbelieving Jews. These people were extremely angry because Paul and Barnabas were preaching that Jesus was the Son of God. The Messiah. It was a spiritual "in your face" if you will. Paul and Barnabas were then—as they say—unceremoniously shown the door. Translated: they were kicked out of town. And it wasn't pretty.

In fact, it may have been violent. All the Bible says is they were "persecuted" and driven from the region. But did they quit? Absolutely not. Even though they could have made a strong argument for throwing in the gospel towel. Pain and ridicule get old quick. Instead, however, the Scripture (Acts 12:51 NKJV) says, "But they shook off the dust from their feet, and came to Iconium." As little Sonya Pursehouse would do, they went on to the next willing listener.

Paul and Barnabas set the example for all Christians. When met with rejection and dejection the message from these two brothers is: don't quit! Rather, move on and look for the next opportunity to stand for Jesus Christ. Look for the next opportunity to tell someone about His love and redemptive power.

THESE THREE THINGS

1. Be prepared for rejection from others—even family—when you stand for Jesus Christ.

2. Concerning the gospel, the messenger is not responsible for how the hearer responds. (Too many Christians carry this false guilt.)

3. Don't tell your eight-year-old Girl Scout daughter, "Records are made to be broken."

OFF THE RECORD

"Okay, okay,
best two out of three."

–Jonah to shipmates

Psychic Police

Have you ever just wanted to call up one of those psychic hot lines just to see what all the fuss is about? Or maybe just to harass the person on the other end of the line.

"Hello. Yes ma'am, I have a little problem and I saw your number on TV and decided to give you a call. Am I being charged now? Okay, so, like, I know this sounds strange, but I think I am a cat trapped inside a man's body and I have this uncontrollable desire to purr and meow in public and it's causing serious problems between my wife and me. . . Hello?. . . Hello?. . .I thought you had hung on me there for a minute. . .Hello?. . .Ma'am, I am a cat inside this human body and I want out. Do you hear me? Please, tell me what I need to do. I'm desperate. Give me some answers. I'm paying good money for this and I want my litter box back.

Help meeeooww here!"

I know, I know, harassment is not a Christian virtue. Still, there's a side of me that would love to do this.

Seriously, so-called fortune-telling and predicting the future has become big, big business in the United States. Many of the same people who dismiss the Bible have no problem calling 900 numbers to talk with someone they don't even know in search of what tomorrow holds. Or they may turn to the horoscope in the morning newspaper to find the same answers.

Recently, I read the following newspaper article about a police chief in Camden Point, Missouri:

This small town's police chief has resigned amid charges he made $20,000 in calls to a psychic hot line at taxpayer expense.

Thomas J. Tobin, 35, allegedly made as many as 280 calls from September through December. He was arrested by sheriff's deputies January 3 and charged with stealing by deceit, a felony.

Question: If this psychic is so good, why didn't she warn Chief Tobin he was about to be busted?

By the way, when you call one of these lines, do you get one of the fifty sub-psychics holed up in a cubicle filing her nails? Or do you get the big-dog psychic in the front office? As a consumer, I think these are legitimate questions. Maybe the more you pay, the higher up your call goes.

The econo-psychics or entry-level psychics are for those callers who want to know a little about their future but who are too cheap to pay much for it. Then, if you want to move up and pay a little more, you can talk with a management-level psychic who will give you more options in terms of what you want to hear. First you'll get the menu.

"If you are on a Touch-Tone phone, use the following selections. If you're not on a Touch-Tone phone, you really don't have the money to be calling our service. The first thing you need to do to brighten your future is step out of the Dark Ages and get a Touch-Tone phone. Please.

"Now, for those of you with a Touch-Tone, for romance, touch one, for finances, touch two, for general feel-good predictions, press three. . ."

However, if you have a VISA gold card and Touch-Tone phone you can talk to the big-dog—or in the South that would be big-dawg—psychic between the hours of two and four P.M. The rest of the time she's taping shows with Dionne Warwick and counting money. And if the former Chief Tobin is any indication, she's counting a lot of it.

Contemporary Christian artist Carmen sings a song titled "America Again" where he proclaims, "You don't need to look to the stars to guide you, when you can look to the very one who made those stars."

The Word of God condemns (although not politically correct, we will be using the "C" word in this book) fortune-telling, soothsaying, and all forms of witchcraft (2 Chronicles 33:6, Galatians 5:19–21). I have to admit, this is an area I absolutely do not struggle with at all, and so I tend to laugh it off. However, we live in an age where many people around us find curious "spiritualism" or "psychic phenomena." As Christians, we need to be ready to answer the claims of those who follow New Age beliefs of any type. We need to challenge others to examine the claims of Jesus Christ. In fact, most New Agers proudly claim to be "open-minded" and willing to explore any and all religions. Challenge the New Ager to explore the Gospel of John and then discuss it with you.

One minor detail: We had better be ready to discuss Jesus Christ with them. 1 Peter 3:15 says: "But sanctify the Lord God in your hearts, and always be ready to give a defense to everyone who asks you a reason for the hope that is in you, with meekness and fear" (NKJV). If indeed you are a Christian, do you know why you have put your trust in Jesus Christ?

Well, I hope someone shares Jesus with Chief Tobin. I guess the only possible out for him—that is, if truth weren't an issue—is to claim he was testing the psychic service to see if it could help him solve unexplained crimes in Camden Point.

Camden Point? Unexplained crimes? How much spending can you justify attempting to find out whose dog dug up Mrs. Jones's flower bed? Or maybe it was a cat? Which means, maybe it was me. Who knows?

MEOW!

These Three Things

1. Psychics, horoscopes, and other New Age phenomena are condemned by God and should not be a part of the Christian's life in any way, shape, or form.

2. The Christian should be prepared at all times to share and defend his or her faith in Jesus Christ as the Savior of mankind and Lord of the universe.

3. Harassment—however fun and tempting it may be—is not a Christian virtue.

OFF THE RECORD

"Hey, what about Mary?
She's got a good voice."

–Peter to Paul

NO MORE MR. NICE GUY

When I was growing up, one value my mom tried to impress on me was kindness. "Be nice to others," she would say all the time. "Be friendly," was another of her daily reminders. She was also proud that Mississippi—our home state—was known as the "Hospitality State." When I reminded her about another lesson she taught me—that it was wrong to be proud—she tried to explain to me the difference between good pride and bad pride. I told her I loved her, but, she was confusing my little mind and my friends were waiting on me. Momma would often bite her bottom lip at this point and bottle up her true feelings towards me.

Well, Momma would not like what happened recently in Detroit, Michigan. No sir, she wouldn't like it one bit. It seems city police officers have been ordered not to say "Have a nice day" to citizens anymore. Honestly. It seems many Detroit citizens were offended by the universally recognized friendly saying. Especially when uttered by an officer issuing a citation.

You folks in Detroit need to lighten up. Really. If this becomes a trend, "See you later" will soon be interpreted as entrapment.

But wouldn't you have loved to be a fly on the wall at that morning meeting when the police captain came in and spoke to his officers informing them of the new policy:

"Okay. Here's today's report, ladies and gentleman, so listen up. We've still got the drive-by shootings going on the north side, there's a new gang in town called 'Dead Blue,' with us as their primary target, and the main artery into town will be closed from three to six P.M. this afternoon, so be ready to be cussed by one out of two citizens while directing traffic. And, oh yeah, I almost forgot, there's a new order from the chief's office for us to quit being nice to people. Anyone caught being nice to any citizen, black or white, male or female, young or old, will have to deal with me. And I will not be nice to you when you come into my office. This is serious business, officers. The chief, the mayor, the city council, and the entire citizenry of Detroit are counting on you not to be nice to people anymore. Now, are there any questions? Good. Now let's see some scowls and hit the streets."

I can just see it, later that day when officer Johnson is called into the captain's office. Johnson sits down as the captain looks out the window and begins to talk, his voice cracking with emotion.

"Johnson, this is difficult for me to talk to you about, but it's my job. I understand you were seen being nice to a little old lady crossing Third and Main this afternoon. I. . .I. . .I didn't want to believe it, Johnson, but they've got a. . .they've got a. . .well, there's a videotape that will be played for all of Detroit to see on channel six tonight with you clearly saying, 'Have a nice day.'

"You've been a model police officer for seventeen years, Johnson, and now this. Don't you have anything to say for yourself, Johnson?"

Really. If I can have a word with you folks from Detroit for just a second. If you don't mind, move in a little closer so that you can hear me whisper, LIGHTEN UP, PEOPLE!

In Proverbs 15:1 the Bible says: "A soft answer turns away wrath, but a harsh word stirs up anger" (NKJV). Today, it has gotten so that many people make fun of—or take advantage of—those who express genuine kindness.

Jesus Christ was a kind and gentle man. He was nice, respectful, and compassionate. These characteristics were not a sign of weakness, rather, they were signs of love and strength.

For some people these traits come naturally. For others, for whatever reasons, they must be acquired. Christians are being watched by the world around us. If we cannot be kind and gentle towards others—even in trying times—then we are poor witnesses for Christ.

Besides, Momma wouldn't like that. She'd probably bite her bottom lip.

THESE THREE THINGS

1. Kindness and gentleness are virtues of strength and fruits of the Holy Spirit's indwelling.

2. As Christians, we are observed by non-Christians daily to see how we treat others and respond to adversity.

3. There are times in life when it's best just to bite your bottom lip. (Especially with children.)

"What to do with a teenager?"

–King Solomon

Don't Look at Me

One August afternoon I was in our front yard pitching the baseball to my then four-year-old son Wesley while he tried to hit it with his bat. He loves for me to play ball, any kind of ball, with him. I would toss the ball from ten feet or so and he would swing just as hard as he could, but this time, again and again, he was missing the ball. After fifteen minutes or so, I looked at Wesley—knowing that he had hit the ball well the last time we played and that he had a genetic advantage over your average four-year-old—and asked, "What's the problem? Why can't you hit the ball?"

Immediately, and with a "how dare you ask me that" tone in his voice, Wesley replied: "You not (that's right, *you not*) throwin' ball where bat is."

"What?" I said as I processed his words. *You know, that's not a bad comeback from a four-year-old who doesn't use verbs,* I thought. I really didn't know how to respond. In all my years in baseball, I had never heard that one before.

I can just see this excuse catching on in the Big Leagues. I can just hear a Cardinals slugger going back to the dugout after being struck out by Greg Maddox: "You saw it, coach. I put the bat right out over the plate and Maddox completely missed it. I don't know why you're looking at me; your problem is right out there on the mound."

Why is it that we human beings have such a difficult time taking responsibility for our own actions? Why do we have such a hard time accepting blame when we do something wrong or when something we attempt fails? Passing the buck is as old as the Garden of Eden.

One of my worst memories from my five years at Pierce Street Elementary School in Tupelo, Mississippi, was the day I decided to rebel against authority— The Man, if you will—who was always trying to keep us kids down. The Man was Mr. Harry Armstrong, the principal. One of the ways The Man (who, in retrospect, was a really nice guy only doing his job) oppressed us kids was to not allow us near the Purnell's Pride chicken truck when it came around once a week to deliver food—namely chickens—to our cafeteria.

"Let me remind you, students, to stay away from the chicken truck during recess," Mr. Armstrong would say over the intercom. He said this often. "This could be dangerous and someone could get hurt."

One day during recess three other third-grade rebels—Greg, Jim, Eddie—and I decided to unshackle the chains of repression and take a step on the Wild Side. The refrigerated chicken truck had arrived—which was about the size of a large U-Haul—and the driver had opened the doors to the back and gone inside the cafeteria.

"Well, there it is," said Jim. "Well, are we or aren't we?"

"Let's go," said Greg.

"Yeah, let's go over there and see what's inside," said Eddie.

I remained silent but decided I too would see what lurked in the back of the forbidden chicken truck. So we snuck over from the playground to the back of the truck and looked in. Lo and behold, what should we find but a truck full of frozen chickens! In the back of a chicken truck! Imagine that!

"So, this is what the inside of a chicken truck looks like, it's slap full of frozen fowl?" I said.

"Fowl?" said Jim. "I don't smell anything." I was always the one with the advanced vocabulary. That's why I'm a writer and the others are making a lot of money with jobs that don't require complete sentences. This is how my friends make a living now:

"You need?"

"Not sure."

"Oh, you need!"

"How much?"

"Not much."

"Come down?"

"A little."

"Okay."

"Sold!"

Or something like that.

Well, as fate would have it (or predestination for you Presbyterians), the cafeteria manager and truck driver came out and caught us dead-to-rights. (What does this term mean? I have no idea, but I've heard it all my life.) Yes sir, we were in the very act of standing around looking dumb in the back of the Chicken Truck.

I just stood there dumbstruck. There's nothing you can do or say at this point. I mean, we're in the back of the strictly-off-limits chicken truck while our classmates are on the playground and the mean old cafeteria lady is staring right at me. I couldn't run. I couldn't, like, say, "Oh, look over there, Johnny

Wilson's throwin' dirt clods at little Missy Lane again," and then jump out of the truck. The oldest trick in the book, that of distraction, wouldn't work at this point. No way. I didn't even think about it anyway. I just stood there waiting for her to do or say something bad.

"Children, to the office now!" said the mean old cafeteria manager, a lady whose name I've long since forgotten. My heart started to pound at the thought of what our punishment might be. Forget "our," I was worried about *my* hide. What to do? What to say? Who could be the fall guy for us? Surely Greg, Jim, or Eddie would be a man and take the blame so all of us wouldn't have to get a whoopin'. John Wayne would. I would have, but my daddy was a preacher. My daddy was "Brother Don," pastor of Lee Acres United Methodist Church just a mile from the school. I couldn't be responsible for turning these other three kids, whose dads had pagan jobs, into juvenile delinquents and have this put on my Permanent Record and disgrace my dad and our family! This would kill my sweet momma. Just kill her.

I tried begging, pleading, and everything else to avoid going to see Mr. Armstrong. "Did I ever tell you you make the best fried chicken in the South?" I lied, looking up at the mean old cafeteria manager as she escorted us down the long, long hallway to The Office. "Forget the South, how 'bout the world? Really, I've eaten a lot of fried chicken in my day and I'm tellin' you, yours is absolutely the finest. Colonel Sanders couldn't lick your lard, ma'am."

My false flattery didn't work. There we stood in the office before The Man himself.

"Mr. Armstrong, these young men were up in the back of the chicken truck, I caught 'em dead-to-rights," said the mean old cafeteria manager lady.

"Did, huh?" said Mr. Armstrong sternly, looking at the four of us in a single-file line. I was the tallest—or at least felt that way—and my neck was sticking out like a "hey-look-at-me-I-did-it" giraffe. "Caught 'em dead-to-rights, did you?"

"Yes sir, dead-to-rights."

"Well, boys, we've been over this rule a thousand times, haven't we now?"

I began to look away and scratch my head as I pondered the honesty of this statement. A hundred maybe, but a thousand? Should I challenge this, prove The Man wrong, see if he wouldn't back down a little while scoring a few points with the boys in the process?

"Mr. Wildmon, look at me when I talk to you, son."

Nope. Bad idea.

"Yes sir."

"Well, now, you boys weren't just caught now, were you? You were caught dead-to-rights."

This sounded worse than just your basic case of getting caught, I thought. We had been caught dead-to-rights, which obviously was a very, very bad way to get caught. I began to wonder, *Why hadn't my parents ever told me about this dead-to-rights thing? Why was The Man using the word "dead" so much here? Did he have the authority to carry out capital punishment?*

Well, we each confessed to the obvious, repented, and received one swift, not-so-friendly reminder to stay away from the chicken truck before we returned to the friendly confines of the playground. But the important lesson I learned that day was I needed to be quicker on my feet with creative excuses when caught doing something terribly wrong like climbing up in the chicken truck. So that about wraps up this story and. . .

What? Excuse-making and blaming is the American way, no? Actually, the very valuable lesson made clear to me that day was that there were consequences to my actions and when I had done wrong, it was better just to confess, come clean, and not try and make excuses—often dishonest excuses—for my wrongdoing.

In Genesis chapter three, Adam and Eve disobeyed God and ate fruit from the forbidden tree. Now, the Scriptures say Eve gave the fruit to Adam and he ate it. Adam could have said no to Eve. But he chose to say yes. Adam was responsible for his own disobedience, yet when the Lord confronted him, the Bible records Adam's response: "The woman you put here with me, she gave me some fruit from the tree and I ate it."

A 1990s American male might answer the Lord this way: "Yeah, I ate it, but this woman you put here with me (finger pointing) made me do it. If you want to blame somebody, blame her and leave me out of it."

I didn't have to teach Wesley how to blame someone else that summer's day. It came naturally.

Often, instead of just 'fessing up when we goof up, mess up, blow it, or—dare I say it—sin, we just find someone or something to blame. You do, I do, we all do. This mind-set has had devastating effects on the American family.

Newsweek magazine had a recent cover picture of a seven-year-old black boy with the words, "A world without fathers: The struggle to save the black family."

These young men—and sometimes not so young—who are responsible for these children are shirking their responsibility or blaming someone for why they aren't fathering and providing for their children as they should. This and other problems caused by irresponsibility happens all to often among white men as well.

I am certainly not saying circumstances, environment, and other outside forces aren't factors—sometimes major factors—in the problems our society faces and in the reasons why individuals do things that are wrong and irresponsible. But what I am saying is that we need to be more willing to say so when we're wrong and accept responsibility—or blame—when we should.

One day we will all stand before God and there will be no shirking, no blaming, and no running away from our own lives.

Well, I guess Wesley will learn more clearly how to accept responsibility in a couple of years when he swings and misses three times in a real game, and the umpire yells, "Strike three, you're out!" and sends him back to the dugout. In the meantime, dear old Dad will work on him as the Lord God works on me.

Now, when to tell him about dear old Dad and the chicken truck escapade? It wasn't actually my fault, you know. I just kind of got mixed up with the wrong crowd and, well, one thing led to another and then there was this giant frozen chicken that came to life. Yeah, that's it! Now, I'm not talkin' your average giant frozen chicken, oh no. No, no. I'm talkin' a Big Bad Boneless Giant Frozen Chicken that could whoop Godzilla without any problem and would terrorize the other children if not for me and my buddies. . .

THESE THREE THINGS

1. Whether we will admit it or not, we all fail God and those we love. We should be willing to take responsibility for our own actions, regardless of the actions of others. Avoid the blame game.

2. God doesn't have any grandchildren. One day, we all—individually—will give an account for our lives before our Maker. What will you say?

3. I suppose I need to provide evidence that it is my genetic heritage that gives Wesley an athletic advantage over other children his age. But you know, those DNA tests are expensive. . .

"Nothing personal,
but I really don't want
to hear your problems."

–Job to his neighbor

White Line in the Storm

Most of us have been through earthly experiences that God used to teach us spiritual lessons. (If you have had an experience somewhere other than Earth, please send me your account for my next book. For this book though, I'm sticking with experiences below, let's say, oh, the ozone layer.) The Lord Jesus used experiences of day-to-day living to explain many of the things of God. Today, we call those stories Jesus told parables. Well, I guess you might say a personal parable happened to me some time ago, and I'd like to share it with you.

Before I came on board at American Family Association, I worked as a sports reporter at a newspaper in Columbus, Mississippi, about sixty miles southeast of Tupelo. The job didn't pay much, but I enjoyed my work. I have always enjoyed sports and I have always enjoyed writing, so sports journalism came naturally to me. Up until our third child Walker was born, I still enjoyed moonlighting covering football and basketball games.

One Saturday night I was leaving the coliseum on the campus of Mississippi State University after a basketball game; a strong wind was blowing, and I could hear thunder in the distance. I recalled hearing a couple of other reporters talking about the stormy weather; one even said he would spend the night instead of trying to brave it. The skies to the north did look real nasty.

As I reached the highway, I turned the radio dial, stopping on a station that was giving the latest weather report. The announcer told of a severe storm moving through the area and began to describe how fast it was moving and the intensity. I realized, with little doubt, that somewhere down the road I would intersect with that storm before I made it home.

Well, I got about halfway home without much happening. However, I noticed an awesome display of lightning ahead of me as I drove closer to the storm. Why didn't I stop at that point? I don't know, except that the old male ego got in the way and I wanted to get home. I ask the same question of people who choose to live in Minnesota. Why would you do it, knowing the kind of brutal winters you're going to have to suffer through? (And although I've polled several of my buddies who live in the Land of 10,000 Frozen Lakes, I've yet to get a logical answer.) But by this time, it was after midnight and I would have felt stupid just stopping. Mother Nature was going to have to show me that she meant business, and guess what? She did.

A few more miles down the road it hit and it hit hard: strong winds, booming thunder, near-blinding lightning, and the hardest rains I can remember driving through. I got a little scared; my heart beat faster and my hands made a death grip around the steering wheel as I realized the situation I faced on this rural, two-lane highway. The rain was so hard that all I could see was the white line on the side of the highway. That was it. I could not even see if there was a shoulder where I could pull off and wait it out.

My eyes were fixed on that white line as I moved very slowly. I may have blinked once in fifteen minutes. What seemed like gale force gusts of wind shook the car. But I kept moving very cautiously, and I finally made it into the city after about thirty minutes of high-stress driving. I was perspiring profusely, but the rains finally halted and I drove on home.

While pulling into my carport, I thought about how important the white line was to my safety, to my very life. I had never really thought about it before. Someone painted that white line long before I found myself in that storm. Without it, I very well could have driven off the road and into a ditch or into the other lane and been involved in an accident.

Translating that into my Christian faith, the white line I depend on is the Holy Bible, the Word of God. Men inspired by the Holy Spirit painted it a long time ago and it has guided millions of people like me since.

When the storms of life come—even if we find ourselves right in the midst of them—we can bank on the Bible as truth, the way through the storm. We can put our assurance in the promises of God found in the His Word, even if we can't see what else is in front of us. It's called faith and, yes, sometimes it's blind. Sometimes we can't see or know exactly what's down life's road. But we can know this: God will be with us no matter what lies ahead.

THESE THREE THINGS

1. Always look to God's Word—the Holy Bible—when confronting life's storms.

2. "Thy word is a lamp unto my feet, and a light unto my path" (Psalm 119:105 KJV).

3. As evidenced by my insistence in driving right into the teeth of the storm, the male ego is a stubborn beast to tame.

OFF THE RECORD

"Why have you clammed up on me back there all of a sudden, honey? . . .Honey. . .honey. . .hon?"

–Lot to his wife

ARE WE HAVING
FUN YET, DAD?

"When life hands you a lemon, make lemonade," someone very important once said. Perhaps it
was Jack Lemmon, I'm not sure. Indeed, one of the
greatest challenges for Christians is taking a bad experience and turning it into something positive. In a
greater spiritual sense, the Bible tells us the Lord
works all things together for good for those who love
Him and are called according to His purpose. God
can take what's wrong and make it right.

I've had a few bad experiences in my life. Some
serious and others trivial. Let me share with you a
trivial pursuit from the Wildmon family album that
turned as sour as—well, excuse the pun—lemonade.

I love nature. I love seeing, breathing, and touching God's majestic handiwork. The Colorado Rockies,
the pristine beaches of the Florida Panhandle, the

cornfields of Nebraska, the bluegrass of Kentucky, or the pines of my own piece of God's country in northeast Mississippi, I love it all. I've been fortunate to have seen most of America, Europe, and Israel, but nowhere on Earth compares with all the natural beauty and lovely variety with which the Lord has blessed America. Even the desert of Arizona has its own beauty.

Yes, I love nature and the outdoors. At the same time—and I say this with apologies to all camping enthusiasts—I hate camping. I really do. I'll tell you why.

A couple of years ago—and it pains me to recall this story, but I'll try—Alison and I were out shopping and ran into friends we don't see very often, Jim and Kim Reese. Jim and I used to ride bikes together when we were ten. We grew up together and still hold the world record for most all-nighters playing Monopoly. After a few minutes in the superstore our conversation drifted into the, "We need to get together" mode. This usually serves as a friendly "good-bye" until the next time you see these same folks, when you will again part with, "We need to get together sometime."

However, during this particular conversation—for some reason—I heard myself asking our friends to block out a weekend and we would go on a camping trip together. I figured our children—then five and four—were at the age when we needed to do the camping thing (or "campin' thang," depending on where you live.) You know—the great outdoors, sitting around the fire roasting marshmallows, doing a little fishing, a little waterskiing, and going to sleep with nature's music. That, after all, is the romantic idea of camping, isn't it?

Well, we agreed on a weekend, and Alison and I began to prepare for this time of rest and relaxation. Tent? Check. Lantern? Check. Sleeping bags? Check. Etc., etc., etc., check, check, check.

After preparing and packing for two weeks, we were ready to go. We were actually looking forward to this weekend of memory making. The campsite was forty-five minutes away, so Alison decided to drive up Friday morning and pitch the tent with our two little angels to assist. I would work until noon and then bring the boat on up.

As I made my way up the Natchez Trace Parkway, excited about the weekend ahead, I began to notice a few dark clouds here and there. Now, during the summer, Mississippi weathermen give the same forecast day after day: "Hot, humid, and a chance of late afternoon thundershowers." So, I didn't think too much about it.

Well, I arrived on the scene to find the tent up, coolers out, and some very hot and sweaty family members. The kids were excited, running wildly about the campsite. Alison, hands on hips and five months pregnant, was acting upbeat. Still, sensitive soul that I am, I sensed a little "I'm not so sure this is a good idea, after all," reservation in her voice as she greeted me. I was just glad to see we weren't at the "This was your great idea, Daniel Boone" stage yet.

Anyway, she greeted me with a kiss and her daily, standard, "You need to talk with your children about _____ (you fill in the blank)." Usually I must exhort them concerning talk or behavior or—in most cases—both.

As we were busy preparing for the evening meal (by the way, when are you not preparing for the next meal on a camping trip?), the dark clouds began to roll in, thunder and all. I thought about what Paul McCartney might say at such a time, but somehow, "Here comes the rain, little darlin'," just didn't seem like it would go over very well with Alison. Besides, I like my jaw just where it is, thank you.

We covered what we could, put several boxes back in the car, and drove around in the rain for a couple of hours. I think it was at this point that we began to think of home—clean, cool, comfortable home. But no, we said, we have planned for weeks, we're all set up, the kids are having fun, and we're not going to let one little rainstorm get to us. So we went back to the campsite and continued preparing the evening meal.

Well, it was about this time that I began building a fire. Can't have a real camping experience without a campfire, you know. The only problem was, I couldn't find any dry wood. But the male ego took over, and I decided I was going to get a fire started if it was the last thing I did. I wasn't going to let any waterlogged wood stop me, no sir. So, I tried and I tried. I blew and I blew. I lit and I lit. After about an hour, my children began to watch with awe, tilting their heads, looking at me as if to say, "Why doesn't our daddy get it? Wet wood won't light. We've known this since birth."

There's a fine line between persistence and stupidity sometimes. And I don't want to know which you're thinking applies to my aforementioned "campfire" exploits.

Later that night we did get a little smoke—after we finished preparing and eating the meal—and a small fire. Really small. But that was okay. We were there to camp and we were going to have fun even if it meant lying to ourselves or pretending to have a good time in front of the kids.

After it got dark, we all decided to sit down in our lounge chairs, let the food settle, and enjoy some good conversation as the kids made mud pies. Just as we were settling in, the first car rounded the corner. Immediately, we were blinded. The little spot we had picked out during the day—the little spot that nobody else wanted now that I think of it—was in the direct path of every car, truck, or off-road vehicle which eased through the narrow park road. At least six or seven times the next couple of hours we would have our privacy ripped away by some joyrider's bright headlights beaming right on us. Like deer, we were. We felt like a live nativity scene, except we were the Little Campers Who Couldn't on display for all to see. I imagined the park ranger was selling tickets for this show. It was awful.

Every time we would sit down and start to relax, *boom*, here came the headlights. We would wave at the people, even though we couldn't see them, because campers are always polite to other woodsmen, you know. Then we would trash them with Christian trash talk. I threw a couple of pork-and-beans cans in the general direction of the cars just to show the children that I was standing up for the family and had had it up to here with this rudeness and inconsideration! I liken it to an evening of constantly having the shower curtain yanked back from you again and again like they do to you at summer camp. I came within a hair of turning my car around to face the road, and shining my brights right back at anyone who drove around that corner—my corner! I got your eye for an eye, pal!

Anyway, after we cleaned the table and put everything away, we bade good night to our friends and climbed in the tent. Fortunately, the kids were already asleep or I would have had to answer questions about why I insisted on getting a campfire started with wet wood. Alison and I made it down without stepping on a child or falling into a tent pole. It wasn't easy.

So there we lay on our backs, nothing between us and nature's floor but a tent and a sleeping bag. (Alison's inflatable mattress had been found leaking earlier in the day and was now a flat and useless piece of plastic. A microcosm of the weekend really.) We began to enjoy a quiet conversation when I noticed—ever so slightly—that blood was going to my head. Although you couldn't detect it while standing, our tent was on a small hump. I tried to downplay it to Alison, talk about other things, but I guess when you're five months pregnant and in a small tent—no rolling over, here—this situation begins to be rather uncomfortable. We did the best we could and slept better than might be expected. Probably because we were completely exhausted. *If the bear comes for the food he can have it,* was my final thought. *Just don't knock the tent down or you and Daddy are gonna tango, my fat furry friend.*

Let me shorten this story by saying breakfast wasn't too hot; the kids were in the poison ivy, ants, and mud;

the boat didn't work right, and I was too tired to fish. Alison got tired of cooking one thing at a time on the little gas stove, I got tired of telling the kids, "Stay away from," and "Stay out of," and we both got tired of swatting flies away from the food. And did I mention how large the mosquitoes grow in Mississippi? Two of them nearly carried little Wesley off!

Well, we decided to bid adieu to our little place in the woods and return home twenty-four hours ahead of schedule. It was a wise and healthy move for the Wildmon family. And yes, it will be a while before this clan returns for more rest and relaxation in the woods.

Although our first—and probably our last—family camping experience was a nightmare in almost every respect, still, we did get to spend this time of trial and error, error and trial, together. We laughed the way worn-out giddy people do on the way home, wondering what else could possibly go wrong? We were making "fun" memories, squeezing lemonade if you will, out of a family adventure that didn't exactly go according to plan. And isn't that the way God works oftentimes?

But I did come up with a new motto which I use whenever asked if I want to take the family camping: As for me and my house, we will serve the Ramada.

THESE THREE THINGS

1. "And we know that God causes all things to work together for good to those who love God, to those who are called according to His purpose" (Romans 8:28 NASB).

2. Finding the good in people—and experiences—that aren't pleasant, is the challenge for Christians.

3. When camping, be prepared to spend 80 percent of your time either preparing to cook or actually cooking.

OFF THE RECORD

"If I have to separate you kids
one more time, I promise you,
I'm turning these donkeys around
and we're going back to Jerusalem!
Do you understand me?!
And you can forget the beach!"

–Jewish dad on family vacation
3,000 years ago

LIFE IS BUT A VAPOR

When Alison and I deboarded the airplane from a trip to Arizona in February of 1993, we were met by her father, our minister, and a couple of friends. We knew something was wrong.

As my father-in-law Jim wrapped his arms around his daughter Alison, he told her that her twenty-five-year-old brother had passed away in the night due to what we later learned was heart failure. It was a paralyzing few moments that will be forever etched in my mind.

Russ and Alison were close. A newlywed and the picture of health, Russ was a Christian and now makes his residence in a place of great joy and peace (Jesus called the place heaven). But when someone so young, so full of life suddenly dies, it serves as a jolting reminder of our own mortality.

The Scripture says our lives are like a vapor.

Our time on Earth is indeed short: Here today, gone tomorrow. We truly don't know what tomorrow holds and as I heard one minister say recently, it's really good that we don't know.

I'm now thirty-five and as I tell my friends, I keep wondering when I'm going to grow up. I'm so weak and immature in so many ways. Jesus taught a lot on priorities and the importance of "growing up" in our faith. St. Paul exhorted us to get past the milk and get into the meat.

During the following weeks and even months after the funeral, people would call or write family members to tell us how much Russ influenced their lives for the better. Some we knew well, some not at all. I thought it very unusual for so many people to make such meaningful comments about someone who lived just twenty-five years.

One of the many things my brother-in-law excelled in was athletics. Russ played college football during the late 1980s at Delta State University in Mississippi and a couple of months after his death, his coach established a memorial award in Russ's name. I drove Alison over for the banquet. We followed her parents. It was a two and a half hour drive from our home in the hills of northeast Mississippi to the flatland area of our state near the Mississippi River known as "the delta." The trip was made longer in ways—and shorter in others—as Alison and I shared a few memories of her twenty-five years, and my twelve years, with Russ.

Alison recalled the time Russ—ever the outdoorsman and always the little brother—tossed a garden snake over the brick wall of their patio one summer's afternoon as she lay peacefully getting a tan. She was fifteen and he was eleven. She was terrified and ran screaming as she heard Russ and his friend laughing uncontrollably. She then regained her senses—somewhat—and did what any big sister would do in similar circumstances—she called her dad at work. Jim tells me this happened on several occasions but by the time he got home in the afternoon, his zeal for bringing justice to the situation had waned. As a dad now myself, I understand this.

Alison also recalled the many times we would drive to wherever to watch Russ play, and he would hug her and squeeze her with his strong, sweaty body after a hard-fought football game. We went all over the South in the fall, and she always told him he was great no matter the final score, what team won, or how he played. He was always the best player on the field, and Alison told him so. He always said thanks with a kiss.

I guess twelve awards or so were given to different players that night, but the coach made the statement that the Russ Hardin Memorial Award is the most important. Why? Because it represented the qualities which Russ exemplified: Hard work, dedication, commitment, dependability, effort, responsibility, good sportsmanship, unselfishness, and good attitude. These weren't trite words but rather powerful and personal words from a coach with whom Russ had spent just two years.

All these made for credibility with Russ's peers and coaches. In short, Russ's life—although short in our way of thinking—touched so many people in such a positive way.

I think the Lord's will for us all is to live our lives in such a manner that when we pass on to heaven, our values and influence for Christ will keep touching lives. Like the pebble's ripple in the pond.

I miss you, Russ. I love you, Russ.

THESE THREE THINGS

1. We should cherish the gift of life here on Earth, for we don't know what tomorrow holds.

2. Each life affects another and another and another. . .

3. For those who know Jesus Christ, a great place of joy, peace, and eternal happiness awaits where we will be reunited with our saved loved ones—and that's no joke.

OFF THE RECORD

"Any questions?"

–Elijah to the prophets of Baal

COSMO WOES

During the Cold War, the United States and Russia took pride in outdoing one another in space travel. We sent a monkey up, Russia sent cosmonauts. We sent John Glenn up, they sent some guy named Vladasmickzk. We sent men to the moon, Russia says it was all filmed in Arizona. It was a competition thing. It was all about national pride.

Well, with the fall of the Soviet Union the Russian space program has suffered in both prestige and in financial support. In fact, a recent event made our Russian friends have to swallow their pride like never before. The following article appeared in the news recently:

MOSCOW—Two Russian cosmonauts will be left in space for forty extra days because the government doesn't have enough money to bring them back to Earth.

It is the second time this year that Russian cosmonauts have been unable to return to Earth on time.

A Russian Space Agency spokesman said that there isn't enough money to build the Soyuz booster rockets needed to bring Yuri Onufriyenko and Yuri Usachev home. American astronaut Shannon Lucid will leave the station as planned on a U.S. space shuttle in early August.

Now, forgive my naiveté here, but isn't this something that should have been worked out before blastoff? I really don't think these guys would have agreed to go had they known.

There are two people in the world that I wouldn't have wanted to be at the time this took place. One is the fellow who had to meet the press, and second is the guy who had to radio Yuri and Yuri the news.

First, the press conference. My guess is the Russian Space Agency went through seven members of the press secretary's office before they finally found someone to do the press conference. The first six said they would gladly go to Siberia for the rest of their lives before they went out and faced CNN and the *New York Times* with the news their country just couldn't afford to bring the cosmonauts down from space.

"Thank you for coming, ladies and gentlemen of

the international press. Would you care for some punch and cookies? We here at the Russian Space Agency have a little announcement to make, but before we do, we would like to take this opportunity to wish all our friends around the world a Merry Christmas and a Happy New Year! Yes, I know it's only May, but you just can't get in the holiday mood soon enough is the way we look at it. And just to show you all here in this room a small token of our appreciation for covering this press conference, we've got this Andy Williams tape we'd like to give everyone. We don't have any, how you say, copyright laws here in Russia, so we basically took one tape and made you all a bunch of copies."

"Excuse me, sir, what was the important announcement?"

"Oh, did I say I had an announcement? Well, well. Actually, it's four little announcements. Now, what were they? Oh yes, I wanted to let you know we will be closed on Friday, a terrible snowstorm has hit Havana, Cuba, we don't have enough money to bring our cosmonauts down from outer space, and we strongly believe the New York Yankees will win the World Series this year. Sorry, no time for questions. Thank you for coming and be sure to pick up your free Andy Williams tape on the way out. Bye-bye, now."

But I have to tell you, I would have much rather

done that, than get on the horn and inform Yuri and Yuri what had befallen them.

"That's a great one, Moscow! Ha! Ha! Yeah, Yuri and I are laughing our heads off. You're laughing, aren't you, Yuri? Oh yeah, we bending over here, Moscow. Now, when you're finished with your little jokes, Yuri and I want to know when we can bring this ship down to Earth. We're exhausted, the toilet's not working right, and if we have to play one more game of Monopoly with the American, I think we'll just lay down and die. Yuri here has gotten to where when he goes directly to jail, not only does he skip passing Go and collecting $200, he just sits in jail. He doesn't care anymore, Moscow. Now, you boys have had your little fun about having no money to bring us home, what's the real story?"

Obviously sufficient plans weren't laid for this trip by our Russian friends. They didn't count the cost before embarking on this mission and this poor planning caused at least two Yuris a lot of grief.

In Luke 14, Jesus spoke of this principle, long before space travel was popular, when He told the parable of the tower and of the king going to war. He said if anyone wanted to follow Him, he must first count the cost. What do we have to give up to follow Jesus Christ?

Sometimes it means we must pay the price of rejection by others. Sometimes even our family and friends will reject us, but Jesus said to be true to Him, we must love Him more than we love our own family. We must love Him more than we love our life. Powerful words. Life-changing words.

I don't know about you, but these are sobering words for me.

Jesus paid it all. All to Him I owe.

Ultimately, to live for Christ means I must die daily to myself. I must first ask what Jesus desires of me and not what I want. I must be willing to count the cost—and pay it—if I'm going to carry out His mission for my life.

Well, the last word out of Moscow was that singer Willie Nelsonvsk was holding "Space Aid" concerts all over Russia to raise enough money to bring Yuri and Yuri home.

And you know that Yuri and Yuri did what any homesick, stranded cosmonaut would do—they tried to bum a ride off Shannon.

"Say, Shannon, you know the space shuttle is coming by in a couple of days to pick you up and everything, and seeing that we've got ourselves a little problem with transportation and all, well, me and Yuri here were just wondering. . ."

THESE THREE THINGS

1. Jesus said in Luke 14:27: "And whoever does not bear his cross and come after Me cannot be My disciple" (NKJV).

2. Jesus paid the ultimate price for an eternal relationship with you and me. Read John 18 and 19.

3. When planning space travel, stick with the Americans. I mean, we got our faults but. . .

OFF THE RECORD

"I'm tellin' you, son,
you'll never get a job
till you cut that hair."

–Samson's dad

THROUGH THE
GENERATIONS

Turning thirty really made me think about my little world and the greater world around me. Up until this point, I had never really stopped to think about my age and what this milestone meant.

Just ten short years before, I wasn't married, had few responsibilities, was struggling to make it through college, and had no children. As I prepared to jump the thirty hurdle, I had been married almost nine years, I had a cart full of responsibilities, had two children, and another in Alison's womb. Surely—I thought —there are no decades ahead that will bring such dramatic change as has this one. Now, as I move into my midthirties, I'm wondering if this isn't the decade that will bring the most change instead.

After all, the hairline continues to recede at an alarming rate, the struggle to stay in my size 36 pants is constantly before me, my daughter is wearing a training bra, we've got something going on almost every day of the week from baseball to church to yard work and—to top it off—I'm now executive vice president of a national Christian ministry with a hundred people under me.

Whew! May I get off this ride for a few weeks? Nothing fancy, just a nice break of no worries or troubles for a couple of years right now would be nice. I know—how well I know now—it just doesn't work that way.

I have determined to build my personal and my family life on the moral values that come from the Holy Bible, the same ones that served this country so well for so long. I guess you could call me "old-fashioned" at the ripe old age of thirty-five. Some of my contemporaries call it being "out of touch with reality." A spokesperson at the White House recently called my type "uneducated and easily led" or something to that effect. (Sometimes I wouldn't mind being uneducated and easily led, I'll be honest. It might make life simpler.)

A while back I was in a meeting with three folks in their late fifties. One of them made the comment —and I think correctly so—that the main problem with my generation is that we've never had to suffer.

The other two nodded their heads in agreement and said amen. The gentleman meant that statement in the sense that—for the most part—we've never had to want or do without, and in most cases the necessities and even luxuries of life were handed to us on a silver platter. *You know, for the most part, he's right,* I thought. (At this point, I could tell by their body language the "hard-times-you-ain't-seen-nothing-boy" stories were cocked and ready, so I didn't engage the three in an argument. Not that I really wanted to.)

I kind of chuckle when I hear my mom and dad talk about schools letting out in the fall so the kids could go into the cotton fields of the hill country in northeast Mississippi and pick cotton to make harvest. God knew when to born me, I assure you. After five minutes in one of those cotton fields I'd be whining, complaining, and crying for Momma.

In his autobiography *Right From the Beginning,* Pat Buchanan writes: "To my mind, the quiet men and women of my parents' and uncle's generation, who survived the Depression and carried our country through the Second World War, were the finest young generation we have ever produced." They suffered.

Having had the great privilege of a relationship with all four of my grandparents until I was thirty—three have since passed on—I agree with Pat Buchanan.

Those in their midfifties and above remember an America altogether different from the one my generation knows. Some things have changed for the better, such as civil rights for African-Americans, but, morally speaking most have not. The saddest thing of all is that my generation has no real frame of reference with which to compare today's secular—and if I can use a stronger word—anti-Christian society.

During the recent presidential campaign I heard one rather young commentator say that what scared him the most was a member of his generation leading the country. And we were told "character" wasn't relevant anymore. Well, now I'm thirty-five and watching the Christian values of my grandparents and parents mocked and scorned as a new generation of Americans says, "So long, God, we can take it from here."

My fellow Americans, we need to remember the godly heritage of our forefathers and turn back to the almighty God.

THESE THREE THINGS

1. As we can see from the Great Depression
   and World War II, trials and tough times
   in life can actually make us better people
   if we have the right attitude and are
   willing to learn and grow from them.

2. America needs to humble herself and fear
   God once again (2 Chronicles 7:14).

3. The reason men lose their hair is that
   they have too much testosterone—which
   is the male hormone. (I'm not lying, look
   it up.) Which means, the more hair we
   lose, the more of a man we really are!
   Yeah, I know. It doesn't help my feelings
   either.

OFF THE RECORD

"Say, Gideon,
don't take this personal,
but have you had
your head examined lately?"

—One smart-mouth soldier

CANTERBURY'S BIGGEST TALE

Have you ever driven up to a store looking for a parking place and all are taken except one or two way back from the entrance? The mall or supercenter being the worst. At one of the supercenters where Alison and I tithe to the Walton family, when you finally get to the last parking spaces in the lot, they have a sign pointing to the store. In fact, the sign says "Supercenter 2 miles." Right below it is another which reads "Rest rooms, water, and picnic area available at halfway point. Have a nice day shopping with us. Remember, we're your store for convenience." Yeah, right.

But near the front of the store, as you drive up, there are those six empty parking spots right next to the entrance. The ones with blue paintings of wheelchairs. The ones that call your name as you drive slowly by. "Come to mama, my lazy son, come to mama. . ." These, of course, are spaces reserved for the handicapped among us. And they should be. As much as possible we need to accommodate those who have difficulty getting out and about.

But in all honesty, in the rush of things, I'm sometimes tempted to pull into one of these parking spaces. After all, I reason, only one of the six is actually being used. What are the chances of five more handicapped folks driving up in the twenty minutes I'm going to be in the store? Really.

I'm glad to say I haven't given in to this temptation, but in my mind, I have played out the scenario of getting out of my car and limping real bad into the mall. I mean holding my leg and letting out an occasional grunt and the whole nine yards. But again, I've never given in to the temptation of faking disability.

I can sure tell about a man who has. His name is Charles Barry and, boy, did Charles pull a whopper. A big-time whopper. Let me quote from an Associated Press article that appeared in papers recently:

Charles Barry's charade held up for six years. He shaved his head, talked of awful chemotherapy treatments, and told all who would listen that he was dying of cancer.

I realize you know where this is going, but I've got to continue quoting this story. It's too good to miss. Or too bad. Depending on how you look at it.

His ruse finally unraveled, the New Hampshire man pleaded guilty to mail fraud in U.S. District Court, admitting he lied to collect disability checks, the free use of a car, and charitable donations.

"I want to apologize to all the people I've hurt," Barry said. "If they can't give their forgiveness. . .then I'm sorry."

The fifty-one-year-old, divorced ex-car salesman (boy, that profession really needed this for its image) faces up to five years in prison and up to $250,000 in fines, plus restitution, when he is released.

Barry became a well-known figure in Canterbury, New Hampshire, a town of 1,717, where he moved with his family in 1991.

He spoke freely about his kidney, lung, and prostate cancer, prosecutor Arnold Huftalen said. He shaved his head, claiming chemotherapy made his hair fall out, and wore brightly covered bandannas. He also used a cane.

Bless his heart. Charles couldn't fake just one area of cancer, no. He had to have kidney, lung, and prostrate cancer. This had to be really bad. Beyond hope.

Barry attempted to substantiate his lies to his wife and later his girlfriend by dropping red dye into his toilet, claiming to have passed blood in his urine, prosecutors said.

And in 1992 he told people in church he didn't have long to live.

This guy had absolutely no shame whatsoever. None.

His wife at the time, Betty Audet, and three stepsons believed his story, and most residents of Canterbury took him at his word.

Barry collected $135 a week in disability payments from his employer, Grappne Auto Junction, for about three years. He also got free use of a car.

His tale also inspired members of several churches to raise between $20,000 and $70,000 for his purported $1 million worth of medical bills, court records show.

But in March, Barry's girlfriend, Diane Wildfeuer, turned him in after calling the hospital where he supposedly had been treated and discovering he had never been a patient there.

How in the name of New Hampshire's favorite son Bob Newhart, did this guy get away with this for six years? And where did he get the idea of faking terminal cancer in the first place? I can't imagine. *The Twilight Zone* perhaps?

Most of the time when someone fakes or pretends to be something he's not, he at least has an out. There is a point where he can get off the charade train without anyone really knowing or catching up to his act. But there are not a lot of outs when you fake terminal cancer. Sooner or later—and in this case, six years (I'm still amazed) later—your lie is going to catch up with you.

You know, the Bible has a lot to say about lying and deceiving. Both destroy lives, relationships, marriages, families, and in some cases, countries. If you can't trust someone, what do you really have left? We all know people who have suffered the consequences of this sin—maybe it was even ourselves.

Honesty is essential for the Christian. Dishonesty can destroy a Christian witness more quickly than anything I know. Think about it. My mom used to tell me that a good name is a treasure and that I was carrying the name Wildmon and she expected me to uphold our family name. She told me it takes a lifetime to build up a good reputation, but only a fleeting few moments to destroy it. How wise that statement is.

Colossians 3:9 says it directly: "Do not lie one to

another, since you have put off the old man with his deeds" (NKJV).

Most of all, we need to understand that although we can lie to or deceive others—sometimes for years —almighty God sees all and knows all. He knows our heart, our motives, and our intent (1 Samuel 16:7). Always be honest with God. Always be honest with fellow human beings. A clean heart and a good conscience will give you peace like nothing else can.

Don't be like Charles the Charlatan.

THESE THREE THINGS

1. Lying and deceiving are sins and will eventually cause great pain.

2. God forgives all sin and will give you an honest heart.

3. The Little Boy That Cried Wolf has nothing on Charles the Charlatan.

"Hey guys, I've been thinkin'
about this wall thing. . ."

–Nehemiah

HEADACHES
OF THE STOMACH

People need the Lord, Steve Green sings. That's one of my favorite songs. People also need each other. God knew this and it's the reason He created Eve after He looked at Adam and said the poor fellow didn't need to be alone. The Lord also told the couple to be fruitful and multiply. We call this organization—if you will—a family. Family members lean on each other for identity, for love, support, and encouragement. We're supposed to work together. Nowhere can we see how much families depend on each other than on a school-day morning. Please, feel free to bring your video camera into our home and make for yourself a videotape which can be studied for years to come by social scientists as an example of how a collection of individuals of diverse opinions, ages, and hairstyles, can make for a well-oiled machine of togetherness and unity.

Each weekday morning during the school year Alison and I go through the same routine that millions of Americans experience. Six A.M., spring out of bed, dash to the window, pull up the blinds, throw open the window, stick out my head and shoulders and sing out at the top of my thirty-something lungs, "Good mornin,' America, how are ya! Say, don't you know me, I'm your native son! I'm the tr. . ."

"Tim, close the window and quit doin' your psycho routine before the neighbors call the police again," Alison says deadpan as she crawls out of bed.

"But honey, it's my window and their problem. Why, I'm the train they call the City of New Orleans and I'll be gone four hundred miles when the day is done, hon."

"It's five hundred. Now go get a shower, City of New Orleans."

Yes, my enthusiasm and vigor for morning is legendary 'round these parts. Just ask any of the twenty-seven men's small groups I've been through the last five years. I used to come up with creative excuses as to why I didn't make it. The only problem was I could never use them, 'cause they were lies and Christianity frowns on this approach.

"Yeah, well, guys, I really felt like the Lord was

about to speak to me through a dream and I knew you all wouldn't want me to miss out on that blessin' which might have well been about one of you winning the Illinois state lottery even though you didn't play it." Or, "Guys, I got up and dressed and everything. Fixed myself a nice bowl of Kellogg's Corn Flakes, put the standard three spoons of sugar on top, reached into the refrigerator, pulled out the milk, and poured the two tablespoons of milk left in the carton on top of my crunchy cereal—and nearly commenced cussing in my mind. Almost made it to my lips. It was mild and I repented quickly, but nothing ruins my morning like the old surprise-no-milk when my taste buds are all wet and ready to go. So basically, having already put myself in a foul mood, I didn't think it fair to show up at something spiritual and ruin your day as well. You understand, fellas."

"Yes, we understand, Wildmon. You need to do two things for us, brother."

"Anything for you guys."

"One, you need to conquer your flesh and get your fanny out of bed and get up here."

"Yeah, I know but. . ."

"And second, you need to come to grips with your lying."

Actually, when six A.M. rolls around I do what half of America does: I hit the snooze button until 6:27 (ours is set in nine-minute intervals and no, I don't know why). So what? Let ye who has never hit the snooze button throw the first clock radio across the room.

Six A.M., arise (barely), go to the kitchen, and prepare the kids a nice combination of nothing and nothing at all. That's right, I prepare *myself* a bowl of cereal. Alison follows up close behind me and prepares breakfast for our three and while I'm in the shower, they partake of breakfast.

Since the kids are young, we all do our dressing and early morning business in the same general vicinity. The upside of this is we don't have to yell at each other from down the hallway about clothes, books, and the day's plans. Instead, we simplify matters and just yell face-to-face, thus avoiding the communication confusion many American families go through with people spread all over the house, which goes something like this:

"Honey, do you know where the (muffled sound as Dad steps into the closet) is?"

"What?"

"Where did you say?"

"I didn't say. I said (three-year-old turns on

vacuum cleaner and laughs) what did you say?!"

"Did you hear what your mom just said?"

"No, sir."

"Sweetheart, I couldn't hear you and I really need that (clock-radio comes back on because you forgot to turn it off) for work today!"

"What?!"

The downside is working so close together can and often does result in bumping heads, stepping on toes, and toothpaste rinse water being sprayed around, which as any family knows—builds character and strengthens family bonds. I personally have this habit—some would call it a bad habit—of rinsing my toothbrush under running sink water, pulling it up a little, and then running my thumb over the bristles. This often causes water to spray in a variety of different directions, including into the faces of some fellow family members, all over the counter, and all over the mirror Alison spent fifteen minutes cleaning the night before. This really irritates my lovely bride.

But is this something I should have told her about before we married? Is it really something to get all bent out of shape about when many husbands forget to pick their kids up from school and I'm near perfect in every other way? Well, I guess so. Alison considers it a breach of trust in our relationship. I've told her if she can find me one, just one, Gary Smalley book or tape on this particular sin I will consider breaking my little ritual which I think makes a statement more than anything else. It sends a clear message to the rest of the family that dear ol' Dad has finished his personal hygiene business—Old Spice and all—and is ready to lead the family into a new day. I think that's an important message to send my kids in this age of instability, uncertainty, and poor role models such as Dennis Rodman, who probably doesn't brush his teeth at all.

On this particular morning, Alison was fixing Wriley's hair in the bathroom. Both are very particular on how Wriley's hair is positioned for public display and on most mornings this leads to voiced disagreements which I try and stay out of. Momma wants her little girl's hair this way, and daughter wants her hair that way. Me, I've usually got my hands full in the closet, holding my socks to the light to make sure they match. I do this, although truthfully, I don't care too much for matching. In my opinion, matching is overrated.

Who came up with this idea of matching anyway? I've thought to myself many times. I'm personally a believer in the Color Coordination Relativism philosophy, known to most fashion critics as simply CCR. Sigmund Freud, Sir Isaac Newton (although it may have been Wayne), or Cher came up with this I think. *Does God care what colors I wear?* I've also asked myself. No, is the answer I've come up with. (I'm sorry if that doesn't fit your theology. I hope we can still be friends.) However, Alison, on the other hand, is a color-coordinating absolutist. And I never know when she will pull my pants' legs up, do a spot check, and boy, we don't want to get caught mixing black and navy blue, do we? Mix tan and gray and she starts laying clothes out for me the night before.

Actually, sometimes I think it's a good quality to be unpredictable. You know, keep the folks around you guessing a little. It keeps those working for you from getting complacent, is the way I look at it.

"Did you see Tim's cream sock/black sock mix this morning?"

"Yeah, did you see the hole in the ankle? What's that brilliant-idea man gonna come up with today? Any man who can't match his socks must have something more profound on his mind in the morning."

"I don't know, but we better be on our toes because he's probably gonna ask us to be real creative and imaginative today."

Anyway, the boys were on the bed. Walker loves to get on his older brother's back and elbow, squeeze, ride pony, knee, and generally roughhouse Wesley. Most of the time Wesley's good-natured about all this and sometimes even plays along or watches cartoons (or reads his Bible, yeah, that's it) while Walker abuses his body. But, every once in a while Walker will do something like poke Wesley in the eye, which makes my eldest son, well, it bothers him. It annoys him. It upsets him. It makes him talk loudly. It makes him speak in a high-volumned concerned tone. Actually, it can cause Wesley to lash out in anger and threaten to beat his little brother into the mattress and leave him in the box springs. This is where I come in because that's my bed Wesley's talking about and I like my mattress and box springs like they are. Can you imagine trying to sleep with a three-year-old housed in your mattress?

Anyway, while I was making sure right foot was going in right shoe and left foot was going in left shoe, Walker evidently grabbed Wesley around the neck and yanked back really hard, placing Wesley's spine, neck, and head in a very unnatural and extremely painful position. Predictably, Wesley reacted.

"Walker!! Get off me! That hurt bad, lil' boy!" he shouted to his little cotton-top sibling. "You want me to whoop your head right here and now? Is that what you want?!" Then Wesley yelled out as serious as he could be, "Walker, you're giving my stomach a headache!!" I was unable to assist Wes at this time since I was doubled over in laughter at this comment.

You can turn your video camera off now, please. *Please.*

My question is: Just how dysfunctional a family are we?

Sometime crazy mornings around the house are a microcosm of our lives. Running here, hurrying there. Forgot about this, what about that? Everybody seemingly doing their own thing. Spiritual nourishment often left completely out of the equation. There's nothing inherently wrong with being independent, but actually, life's journey is a whole lot sweeter, and more enjoyable, if we look out for one another.

One of the greatest challenges for parents is trying to make all the parts and personalities of a family fit together with some form of cohesiveness, to make the experience positive for the whole, entire family. Balance, it's called.

Well, for those wondering, I stopped Wesley from planting Walker into the mattress. Barely. And we made it to school, as always, 7:35 A.M.

"Mind your teachers, be kind to others, remember

I love you and Jesus loves you. Have a great day!" I say just before they open the car door each morning for another day at school.

Then I wonder on the way to work, Why nine-minute intervals on my alarm clock? Why not seven, eight, or a nice round number like ten? Who decides such matters?

THESE THREE THINGS

1. If each family member will make a concerted effort to honor each other and consider the feelings of each other, it will go a long way in preventing family breakdown and division.

2. The family who prays together, stays together.

3. Can I have that videotape, please?

"The survey results are in, sir.
Half the people in Babylon can't
even spell your name, much less
remember how many times to
bow down and pray to you.
These are busy people, king."

−Advisor to King Nebuchadnezzar

CAN WE FREEZE-FRAME?

"All my possessions for a moment of time."
Queen Elizabeth I, with her dying breath, 1603

They say time flies when you're having fun. I've never been able to figure out who "they" are but I found the saying to be true. In fact, time seems to get away even when you're not having fun. At least that's been my experience.

Springtime in Mississippi generally arrives sometime in mid-March, and this particular year Alison and I were glad to see its arrival. Cabin fever has a strange and sometimes ugly effect on children like ours. A few days, much less a couple of months, cooped up inside with two normally (sometimes abnormally) active children and a baby can—well, let's just be honest here—it can drive an otherwise sane individual crazy. Nutso. It'll make parents say things like, "If I hear another whine out of you I'm going to string you up on that ceiling fan and turn it on full blast and 'round and 'round you'll go, buddy!"

There are only so many things you can build with Legos, and Flipper and Lassie only last thirty minutes each. Yes, call me a hypocrite, but we do use television an hour a day for baby-sitting purposes. I know, I know, this is time that could be spent reading to the children, baking cookies, memorizing Bible verses, or teaching them algebra. I've mentioned all those ideas to Alison on how I would handle it if I were at home during the day. Her response is to tell me what I can do with my ideas, and my response, of course, is to keep other ideas to myself. Have you been there, men? Let me see a show of hands and can you say "Amen!"

Why is it we men—who are supposedly at work dealing with the "real world"—all of a sudden want to give Child Rearing Theory 101 suggestions to our wives when we call home during a mother-child/children confrontation?

"Yeah, honey, have you tried reasoning with the children?

"That's not a good idea, okay, have you set the little angels down on the couch and talked about their positives and negatives? Have you tried using charts, graphs, and other visual aids? Have you tried that approach?

"Okay, okay, settle down, dear. I hear the frustration in your voice. . .oh, that's not frustration, you say. It's raw unadulterated anger. Well, dear, have you called your mother? . . ."

Try as we might, we guys are just not suited to be little Dr. Dobsons over the phone.

Anyway, one beautiful March day I took the kids out in the backyard to play. They both wanted to play on their swing set, so they each sat down and tried to begin swinging. The only problem was that their little bodies had lengthened since last they used the set and now their legs were too long for the seats. Being the observant dad that I am, I went over and raised the seats three notches. Now, this may sound corny to some and ironic to others, but raising Wriley and Wesley's swings was a simple, yet painful task.

While changing the notches, it hit me that my two oldest are growing up. One year closer to adulthood. One year less they will be under my direct care and attention. One year less I will be able to tuck them in at night, talk about the day, say our prayers together, and kiss them good night. For a few short moments, Dad had a lump in his throat. *Man, how time flies*, I thought.

I remember where I was when Alison told me she was pregnant with each child. I remember the words of the pastor as we dedicated each to the Lord. And now our two oldest are starting school and needing the swing raised three notches. It won't be long until the swing set won't be fun anymore. Can we freeze-frame here?

Well, that gorgeous March afternoon served as a reminder that I have only a few short years left to shape and mold my children into what God intends them to be, and to create fond memories for them of their early years at home.

My, how time flies.

God bless the children.

THESE THREE THINGS

1. Time is a commodity given to us by God. Use it wisely.

2. As Steve Green sings, children are a treasure from the Lord.

3. Did you ever notice that the old Flipper shows always used the same three scenes of Flipper in the water? Every show, same three shots all through the show. One shot of him on his tail, one shot of him swimming, and one shot of him jumping out of the water. On second thought, I don't know for sure Flipper was a male. Bottom line, this fish was terribly over-rated and did not earn his money!

AFTERTHOUGHTS

Well, friends, we have come to the close of the book. It's kind of sad, isn't it? We've gotten kind of close, you and I. I've let you into my world, been vulnerable and transparent, and you, well, you haven't said a thing yet. Nothing. You've just sat there with your nose in this book. I've been wondering when you're going to open up and get real with me. Use me as a sounding board, I don't care, just talk to me. Go ahead. Take the book just like you have it now, place it up against your face, and talk to me. Come on, for once in your adult life, be free and uninhibited. I don't care if anyone looks at you and may think you need professional help, just tell them what this book has meant to you and they'll understand. If not, just begin repeating your multiplication tables over and over and they'll soon leave you alone.

You know, I'm so glad that God gave us the "sixth" sense of humor. Really, laughter to me is just as important as smelling, tasting, seeing, feeling, and hearing, otherwise known as the five nonhumorous senses. (Although I've seen some funny-looking noses in my day.) As I mentioned in the introduction, great health benefits come from regular, daily doses of laughter. No doubt, the Lord made His children this way.

Let me encourage you to find ways to laugh, especially at the one in the mirror. As my Mama Wildmon used to say—God rest her soul—"Tim, shut the door behind you, son! Were you raised in a barn?" Wait a minute, that's not what Mama Wildmon used to say. Actually, she told me many times something I've never forgotten. She said in her sweet voice, "Life's too short to take everything so seriously. You got to stop and smell the roses along the way."

Now, to answer the question, what did Noah do with the woodpeckers? You have been patient in your curiosity, reading the entire book from beginning to end, so I'm going to give you an answer. Unless, of course, you cheated and read this section before reading the rest of the book. In that case, you have sinned and your penitence is to go buy another copy of this book for a friend or family member who could use a little cheer.

Now, about Noah and the woodpeckers, my guess is Noah, being a lifelong Methodist, formed several committees to look into this matter soon after he was instructed by God to build the ark. Methodists, although they have many good qualities, don't like surprises.

One committee recommended Noah go back and

double-check with the Lord. "Now don't insinuate He made a mistake," they said. "Just say, 'You know Lord, the boat's kind of getting full and we've got an awful lot of birds on board. What about leaving one or two off? I don't know, oh, how 'bout, just for instance, oh, let's say, just to play the devil's advocate here, the woodpeckers?' "

Another committee suggested Noah place the parrot family in with the woodpeckers to keep them entertained, thus taking their minds off what comes naturally (that would be pecking holes in wood, of course).

Yet another committee (and Methodists can get away with this, whereas there is absolutely no way Baptists could and remain members in good standing in their church) suggested using a little wine every now and then to keep the woodpeckers somewhat sedated. Noah, being a teetotaler himself, nixed that idea before the party ever began, sensing self-serving motives on the part of these particular committee members, all of whom volunteered to keep the birds company when the wine was passed around.

Well now, what to do? Finally, Noah, tiring of one useless committee recommendation after another, decided he would just sit down and have a man to bird, nose to beak, conversation with the woodpeckers. He told them, as if they were his own children, that for their own good and the welfare of the rest of those traveling on this cruise, he was placing them in the same cabin—at discounted fare of course—with Mr. and Mrs. Skunk. He then explained in simple words even a birdbrain could understand, that these skunks were basically good, fun-loving animals, who enjoyed a peaceful lifestyle, reading John Grisham novels, and—most importantly—a quiet environment in which to travel. But—and Noah strongly emphasized the word *but* at this point—if riled by loud and obnoxious noises, such as half-crazed birds pounding their heads ninety-to-nothin' against wooden hulls of arks for instance, these skunks would change like Dr. Jekyll and Mr. Hyde into evil creatures who would emit the most awful, something-done-crawled-up-in-here-and-died, can't-stand-it-get-me-out-of-here-or-I'll-throw-up-and-keel-over smell, and it would be soooo bad, that Mr. and Mrs. Woodpecker would curse the very day they were hatched for having to take one whiff of this wouldn't-wish-it-on-your-worst-enemy odor.

And you know what, ladies and gentleman? This plan of Noah's worked.

Actually, the Bible doesn't say a word about Noah having any problems whatsoever with the woodpeckers, and so we can only assume that he didn't have any. Although my little scenario is a clever scheme for dealing with woodpeckers, I've still got to think Noah slept on pins and needles. Slippers, duct tape, and candle always bedside, just hoping he wouldn't hear that dreaded sound that all woodpecker caretakers hate to hear in the middle of the night, that of a hardheaded bird's beak knock, knock, knocking a hole in your ark.

There, as I told you, you now have a logical answer to at least one of the questions of the ages. Aren't you glad you read the last page?

ABOUT THE AUTHOR

Tim Wildmon graduated from Mississippi State University in 1987 with a degree in communications. He finished with a 2.1 GPA and is pretty proud of it. Elizabeth Dole spoke at his commencement, but he doesn't know her personally. (You know, like on a first name basis or anything). He is currently the vice president of American Family Association, a Christian organization based in Tupelo, Mississippi. He co-hosts a one hour Monday–Friday radio call-in program, "Today's Issues," on the American Family Radio network and speaks often to church and civic groups all over the country. He appeared on CNN "Talk Back Live" one time as well. Don't forget that because we're talking CNN as in WORLDWIDE television. Wildmon is married, resides in Saltillo, Mississippi and is the father of a daughter and two sons.

Simply put: Tim Wildmon is a great American with much to contribute to the human family. But right now, his attention is on the upcoming football season, so if you are a member of the human family trying to get in touch with him—he'll have to get back with you later to find out what he will contribute. In fact, on second thought, Tim says, he gave to the human family at the office, so go away and leave him alone.

Family tree available upon request.

For more fun and laughter in your Christian walk, contact the Fellowship of Merry Christians, Inc., at P.O. Box 895, Portage, Michigan 49801-0895, or call (616)324-0990.

To contact Tim Wildmon about possible speaking engagements, including retreats, write P.O. Box 2440, Tupelo MS 38803, or call (601)844-5036, extension 231, or email: twildmon@afa.net.